George Nox McCain, Mary V. O McCain

Through the Great Campaign

With Hastings and his Spellbinders

George Nox McCain, Mary V. O McCain

Through the Great Campaign

With Hastings and his Spellbinders

ISBN/EAN: 9783744746977

Printed in Europe, USA, Canada, Australia, Japan

Cover: Foto ©Thomas Meinert / pixelio.de

More available books at **www.hansebooks.com**

Through the Great Campaign

WITH

Hastings and his Spellbinders.

BY

GEORGE NOX McCAIN.

WITH ILLUSTRATIONS AND DESIGNS BY WILLIAM J. GLACKENS
AND MARY V. O. McCAIN.

Souvenir Edition.

No. 315

PHILADELPHIA:
HISTORICAL PUBLISHING COMPANY.
1895.

    This is a book without a preface. More than half a million voters on the sixth day of last November made an introduction unnecessary.

GOVERNOR DANIEL H. HASTINGS.

Twenty-odd years ago, two gentlemen, one of whom was the late ex-Governor Curtin, were walking down the main street in Bellefonte.

"*Do you see that young fellow over yonder?*" *said the ex-Governor to his companion, indicating the direction with a nod of his head. The gentleman by his side glanced across the street and saw a tall, well-built young man, with florid face and upright carriage, marching along, his arm linked in that of a little old lady plainly dressed in black. Her features bore the impress of the cares and anxieties with which a mother's heart, through long years, had been oppressed. It was evident, from the respect which the young man showed toward the little old woman, that she was his mother.*

"*Well, what about him?*" *was the inquiry.*

"*Nothing in particular,*" *continued the ex-Governor dryly,* "*except this, that you want to keep your eye on him. I have known him only a short time, but any man who loves his mother as he does is bound to make his mark in religion or politics. I don't know which it will be in his case.*"

"*What's his name?*"

"*Dan Hastings.*"

"This Man Hastings."

"THIS MAN HASTINGS."

"YOU people who pride yourselves on being self-made American citizens, who glory in the advantages by which you have been enabled to elevate yourselves to the plane of sovereigns, ought to see the farm on which this man Hastings, who heads the Republican ticket, was raised. I've seen it. Its away up yonder among the mountains of Clinton County, and it seems to me that you couldn't raise anything on it but Golden Rod and slate pencils."

It was the eloquent Orlady who swept a vast and sympathetic audience into an uproar of applause at this recital of the humble beginning of Daniel Hartman Hastings.

This farmer's boy, with the sturdy blood of a Scotch-Irish ancestry in his veins, has filled a larger measure of life in the forty-five years of his existence than comes to the lot of most men in any career. Born February 26, 1849, in Clinton County, he received a common school education, became a school teacher, then school principal. Studied law and entered politics and the militia. Became a paymaster first, and then rose through the gradations of service to be Adjutant General. In politics he rose from a county convention delegate to Burgess of Bellefonte. Then a delegate to State conventions, a National Convention delegate with the wide reputation of an orator, finally to become the Governor of the Imperial Commonwealth of Pennsylvania.

Thus in a paragraph is crowded the story of a career whose greatest possibilities are yet in the coming years.

Has Daniel Hastings a war record?

He has.

It is the proud record of a boy of thirteen, fired with the patriotism of the early war years, who, after repeated refusals by his father to permit him to enlist, ran away from the farm one night. He trudged down lonely roads, borrowed wagon rides, and stole his way on railroad trains till he reached Carlisle. His age was against his enlistment without parental consent. Then after all his effort, the father, who knew best, came after the runaway, and carried him back to the farm among the mountains.

At fourteen he began life on his own behalf. He started on borrowed capital and an empty

THE GOVERNOR AND SARAH.

stomach. It was in the winter of 1863. Young Dan was only fourteen. The limited education he had acquired had been gained by the light of "tallow dips" after a day's toil on that farm of Golden Rod and slate pencils. He heard that a school in Wayne Township was vacant. The lad borrowed one dollar, trudged through the snow and secured the appointment conditioned upon his passing an examination. He walked back to Lock Haven the same day, was examined and received his certificate, returning on foot in time to open the school the next morning. His money was gone, and he began life on his own account that day without anything to eat.

Chronologically, here is the story of Daniel H. Hastings' life by years:

1863—County school teacher.
1866—Principal Bellefonte High School.
1875—Admitted to the Centre County Bar.
1877—Paymaster, rank of Captain, N. G. P.
1878—Lieutenant Colonel Fifth Regiment.
1883—Assistant Adjutant General.
1884—Colonel Fifth Regiment.
1886—Nominated Beaver for Governor.
1887—Adjutant General.
1888—Nominated John Sherman for President.
1889—In command at Johnstown.
1890—Candidate for Governor.
1894—Elected Governor of Pennsylvania.
1896—

Some of the details in his later life tell how in the convention which nominated George W. Delamater for Governor four years ago, Daniel H. Hastings on first ballot had sixty-four votes to eighty-four for Delamater. How he declined the chairmanship of the Republican State Committee and was defeated for Director General of the World's Fair by George R. Davis by only six votes out of a total of ninety-four.

General Hastings is a Methodist. A member, with his wife, of the M. E. Church in Bellefonte and one of its trustees.

"I'll never forget my first law suit," he said in one of his campaign speeches. "I was admitted to the bar about ten o'clock in the morning. As I came down from the Court House to my office, I found my first client awaiting me. He had been arrested on the charge of larceny of three pigs. He gave me a retaining fee of five dollars— my first one and badly needed—and we went over to the 'squire's office where the prosecutor and witnesses had gathered.

"At the close of the case I addressed the court. I made a speech, which, at that time, I thought had never been surpassed in the history of jurisprudence in Pennsylvania on the subject of the larceny of pigs. Warming to my subject, I raised my hand over my head, and exclaimed in thunder tones:

"'You cannot, Mr. Justice, under the law and this evidence send my client to prison!'

"The Justice was a Pennsylvania Dutchman, hard-headed and hard of hearing. Leaning on his desk and putting one hand behind his ear, he exclaimed, eagerly:

"'Vot ish das you say?'

"'You cannot under the law and this evidence send my client to prison,' I repeated in stentorian tones.

"'Oh; I can't, can't I?' he exclaimed, rising, very red in the face. 'I can't. Vell, young fellow, yust you set down on dot chair vor a leedle vile, an' vatch me adoin' of it.'"

MRS. D. H. HASTINGS.

A cynical French writer has said, "If you want to see the best side of a man live with him for a week; if you want to see the worst side live with him for a month."

If this be true, then, so far as daily intercourse for six weeks furnishes a criterion, there is no "worse" side to General Hastings. There is not a member of the campaigning party who will not coincide in the statement that no man ever stood up under such continuous strain—six weeks and more of it—and bore it so calmly, with such even temper, with such kindly regard for others as did " this man Hastings."

And nobody but a veteran knows what a campaign means. Four campaigns have taught me that there is no such thing as privacy for the candidate. It is one of the penalties of political preferment. Men of all ages, conditions, character, flock in to shake hands, to congratulate, to condemn, to beseech, to borrow, to advise, to admonish. Every fellow of them imagines that he holds a sight judgment note on the time, talents, and temper of the candidate. They invade his hotel room, sit on his bed, expectorate on the floor, finger his toilet requisites, fill the room with odoriferous cigar smoke and strange oaths, feel the fineness of his clothes, use his pen and ink, read his newspapers and then utilize them as a door-mat ; enter without knocking, and remain without invitation ; peep into his valise, read the superscription on his private mail and do other things calculated to drive the victim into drink or out of politics.

But the General never lost his temper but once. That was at Indiana, where, at 2 a. m., some eager patriot held him up in the hotel hallway and wanted an ante-election pledge that he would appoint somebody to be fireman or messenger or hostler or something in one of the Harrisburg departments. Neither the man or the candidate spoke very loud, but it was opposite my room door, and I was forced to hear. The General said a few things in the calm, dispassionate way a man does when he can't get the stove-pipe joints to fit, and then the man went hurriedly downstairs with the sound as of a thousand of brick coming after him.

There is one subject which the scope of this work permits, but which in its larger sense is barred from the cold lines of newspaper discussion and comment. It is the home life of the man who has been made Governor of this State. To most men in public life home is a convenience. To Daniel H. Hastings home is a sanctuary. It is his city of refuge, the one spot around which all his ambitions, all his hopes for the future, all his successes of the past are centered. Where titles and dignities are laid aside as a garment; where government is personified in a sweet-faced woman and the veto power in the voice of a laughing baby. Where the music of a daughter's song, or symphony, is sweeter than the cheers of listening hundreds, and where the lifted light of God's most gracious gift, love, is brighter than all the Bengal fires and flaring torches that ever burned and blazed in the Great Campaign.

General Hastings' family consists of his wife, Mrs. Jane Armstrong Rankin Hastings, their daughter, Miss Helen, just merging into young womanhood, and little Sarah Fullerton Hastings, aged about thirteen months. General Hastings, no matter what exalted position he may in the future attain, will never appear to better advantage, as a man, a husband and father, than he did on the morning when he stood on the depot platform at Bellefonte, a stop for five minutes in the town, with star-eyed Sarah in his strong arms, his wife by his side, and the crowd pushing and cheering to get nearer to shake his hand.

Hon. Charles Emory Smith, in one of his superb bursts of eloquence found elsewhere in this work, paints the word picture of General Daniel H. Hastings' work at Johnstown as my pen cannot. It is enough to say here, in the brief outline of his life, that, running alongside that black line of all misery, horror and human despair of which Johnstown in 1889 was the climax, there runs the silver thread of General Hastings' patient, persistent and successful effort to restore peace, order and prosperity to the stricken city. History tells that story in detail; I need not repeat it here. Yet all through the campaign, under all circumstances, not a word was uttered or reference made concerning that episode by any member of his party. It was understood that the subject was tabooed in connection with his candidacy and campaign. General Daniel H. Hastings made his campaign on his record of manliness and Republicanism, not on his splendid record in the Johnstown disaster.

General Hastings traveled over 4500 miles in his tour and delivered over 150 speeches. As the central figure in the greatest campaign ever known in Pennsylvania, I have deemed it unnecessary to here give extracts from his eloquent, logical and convincing addresses. The personality of the man and his record of the past speak louder than words.

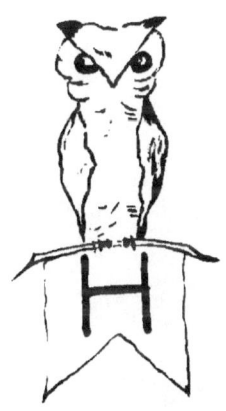

The Spellbinders.

GENERAL JAMES W. LATTA,
Secretary of Internal Affairs.

THE SPELLBINDERS.

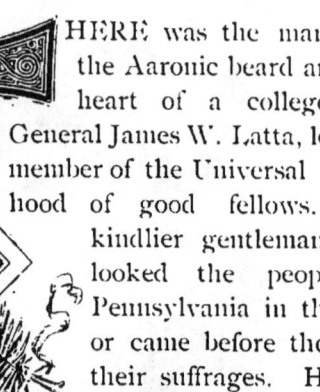

THERE was the man with the Aaronic beard and the heart of a college lad, General James W. Latta, leading member of the Universal Priesthood of good fellows. No kindlier gentleman ever looked the people of Pennsylvania in the face or came before them for their suffrages. He was the one star in the galaxy of the Great Campaign whose lustre never waxed dim so long as the Quartermaster's department was operative.

"Gentlemen, a famous Union general once said, 'An army travels on its stomach.' Now, this party is not an army, but I propose to see that it travels on army principles," he remarked, one morning early in the campaign. Then he bowed his fine head, with one hand on his breast, to the applause of the entire party.

Forthwith, by unanimous consent, he was chosen commissary. Nothing like it was ever known before. A General by right and title made a commissary for a handful of men.

And no man had a better right to the position, for behind James W. Latta was the experience of five long years of army life. Had he not won a commission as Brevet Major in the United States Volunteers' service for "gallant and meritorious action" at Winchester? Had he not been complimented in army orders for gallant service in all the battles before Richmond? And when he was mustered out in Colorado in 1866 as Brevet Lieutenant Colonel and Assistant Adjutant General, had he not served in every department of the army between the Atlantic and the Rockies? He had gone forth, barely out of his teens, into the years of battle. He had heard the music of bullets, the snarl of shell and the thunder-burst of the accompanying batteries in a chorus of carnage.

Here is his record in brief:

Born April 19, 1839. Graduated Philadelphia High School. Admitted to Bar 1860. Enlisted April 19. 1861, Private Company D. 1st Regiment, Pennsylvania Militia. Participated in battles of Fredericksburg, Saline Church, Gettysburg, Cold Harbor, Spottsylvania, Wilderness, etc. Mustered out 1866. Was Colonel of 1st Regiment and Adjutant General, Pa. (for ten years). Is member of Loyal Legion and Past Department Commander of Pennsylvania, G. A. R.

But what a commissary! No army with banners ever had his equal. He knew every good hotel in the State. He was posted on the limits of the pie belt and could define the boundary line of the buckwheat region to a hair's breadth. By virtue of his office and candidacy he always got a second story front room, with bathroom, Brussels carpet and Irish point lace curtains. If there had been any apartment with a private chapel attached, the General would either have pre-empted it or else secured the right to use the chapel. (The General is a Presbyterian by birth and an Episcopalian by association with an estimable Christian wife.)

But Major George B. Orlady, and another member of the combination, worked the "rabbit's foot" on the General out in the western part of the State in a most heartless and disreputable way. There was a great assemblage in the hotel office. Orlady was on the outskirts of the crowd, and from his superb height could see over the heads of all. His eyes were riveted for a moment on the hotel proprietor and his clerk, who were scurrying around behind the desk, their button holes and watch chains gorgeous with secret society insignia. An inspiration seized the Towering Oak of the Middle Mountain.

"Come out of here, young fellow—quick!" he exclaimed, laying a hand on the shoulder of his companion and half dragging him toward the door.

"I am going to see that Latta don't get the best room in that hotel this night, if I can prevent it and there is a God in Israel," he continued with emphasis on the "that," as he shook himself clear of the crowd.

Half a square up street he wheeled suddenly into a cigar store. There was a card full of secret society buttons propped up on the show case. Marks for Masons of all degrees, Knights of Pythias, Elks, Arcanums, Odd Fellows and every other kind of fellows who have grips and winks peculiar to themselves and whose business it is to find some brother in trouble, and then borrow money from him, as the Major puts it.

He bought a supply at ten cents each, stuck one in the lapel of his coat, another in his vest, and gave a couple to his companion in crime to do likewise. Then he fished out of his pocket an emblem and swung it pendant from his watch chain. The buttons were a bright blue, and the contrast with the black ones suggested that the pair had sewed them on in the dark and had got the styles tangled. Back to the hotel went the Major and the other. The proprietor was just checking off the rooms as Orlady, with a voice and smile that had captivated thousands, said:

"How are you? Glad to see you!" and he thrust his fist over the counter. The proprietor took in the gorgeous array of buttons that told him a brother Barbarian and a *Cervus Alces* stood before him. His fingers twisted mystically in a return clasp, while his clerk was going through the same process with the other schemer. That was all.

That night General James W. Latta had a good comfortable room. But it wasn't on the second floor at the head of the stairs, with a twenty-four inch frieze around it, a three-ply Brussels carpet on its floor, and a bed that didn't sag in the middle. Neither did the proprietor send up twice to him to see if all was right; and what time the gentleman would like to be called in the morning—to say nothing of three pitchers of ice water, extra blankets, and something else, with his compliments. Oh, no! But he did that with the conspirators who pulled the covers over their heads that the General might not hear them chuckle in ghoulish glee before they went to sleep.

The General laughed when he heard of it, just as he did over an episode at Kittanning. The night meeting was held in the Court House, the audience packed like sardines in vertical rows. After his speech, the General retired to the judges' room. A man who had listened to the speech with every nerve intent, followed him.

"I'm—I'm goin' to vote for you, Gener'l," said the man in a hesitating bashful way.

"Thank you, sir," replied Latta, beaming through his glasses and shaking hands heartily.

"Yessir, I used to be a dimmycrat, but I'm goin' to vote for you this time, Gener'l Latta," he went on.

"Thank you — appreciate — kindness— sir," murmured the General with his best bow.

"Yessir, I'll never forget you, sir."

The General braced himself for an army reminiscence or a militia episode.

"You signed my pardon to git me out'en the penitentiary, Gener'l."

It was well the grateful man turned away then, for the candidate's equanimity nearly left him. The converted Democratic visitor had mistaken him for ex-Lieutenant-Governor Latta, of Greensburg, at one time a member of the Pardon Board.

———

In his speeches during the campaign, General Latta addressed himself specially and eloquently to his old soldier companions. But he talked tariff, too, as these extracts from his addresses show :

With the stinging official calumny still ringing in their ears "that thousands of neighborhoods have their well-known fraudulent pensioners," the old soldiers of Pennsylvania are urgent to help hurry Democratic capitulation to a speedy political end. They are like a witness I heard of under cross-examination. He had harassed an eminent corporation counsel to testiness. Replying to the counsel's concluding interrogatories, "You have no special affection for the Pennsylvania Railroad?" Mr. Jones said:

"Nothing like so much as you, sir."

So the old soldiers of Pennsylvania have no special affection for the Democratic party, and with a renewal of their patriotic zeal are anxious for active co-operation in every measure and movement that shall tend to assure that party's effectual demoralization and ultimate rout.

I would rather remember the dear old flag, lurid amid the glare, and clamor, and din of battle; I would rather remember it upon the ramparts in the imminent peril of the deadly breach; I would rather remember it as good, old Abraham Lincoln let it float full and free on that crisp, wintry morning in February, 1861, from the dome of Independence Hall, than to remember it when the Paramount Commissioner hauled it down in the Hawaiian Islands; or the Premier weakened its influences in the far Samoan group; or lessened its authority in a near-by Central American Republic. The next time we put it up, we will put it up without halyards; clinch it to the staff; nail it to the spar so that no man with or without authority can or dare haul it down; that it may still forever float with proud significance wherever the seas are the most perilous or the storm rages fiercest.

Down in our city not long since a family of good repute had born to it a fine, bouncing girl baby. After a few days a little brother, some seven years of age, was taken into the chamber to see, for the first time, his newly arrived sister. The boy's acute vision discovered what had not been before observed, the faintest indication of a birthmark upon the little infant's left cheek. He turned to the father, and with much force said:

"Take her back, pop, she's damaged."

The Democratic party had born to it lately a baby, in the shape of the Gorman-Brice-Wilson Tariff Bill. Upon one cheek was stamped "dishonor, ' and upon the other "perfidy." It was taken to the party's father, the President of the United States. He did not send it back, nor did he fondle it with much of a fatherly affection. He permitted it to lie about the house uncared for, and unattended, until it reached the ten day period provided for such babies to reach maturity, when it became a law unto itself. And, as explanatory of his want of care, he said that there would soon, with the next Congress, be another Democratic tariff baby born to this country without the imperfections that had disfigured its neglected sister. But the President counted without his host. The next tariff baby born to this country will be a Republican baby. It will have neither whooping-cough, colds, fever, nor measles. Upon one cheek will be stamped "prosperity" and upon the other "protection."

THE four-word creed of George B. Orlady describes the man. Over the portals of every effort, every ambition, every hope of his life there are written the words, "Love, Home, Country, God." Big bodied, big brained, big hearted; sturdy in his friendships and his faiths, strong in opinion, he merits the soubriquet, the "Big Oak of the Middle Mountain."

The briefest biography of such an one, where dates are concerned, is the best. Deeds and

Major George B. Orlady.

words speak for such as this man, a jurist and a gentleman. This is the story of the past in a life yet full of great possibilities :

Born at Petersburg, Huntingdon County, February 22, 1850. Common schools. Pennsylvania State College. Bellwood Academy, Washington and Jefferson College, August 1869. Studied and practiced medicine with his father, Dr. Henry Orlady. Graduated Jefferson Medical College, March, 1871. Studied law with Samuel Steel Blair, Hollidaysburg. Admitted, January, 1875. District Attorney Huntingdon County, 1878 to 1887. Never held any other office. Married ; three children.

———

His home is his life. Wife and bairns are more to him than anything this side the gates of the unknown. He is a "Shriner" in more ways than one. The one shrine above all others which lifts itself ever into every day of his life, at whose feet he lays all his success of the past and dreams of the future is—home.

Orlady came, with his sunny temperament and eloquent tongue, like a sunburst. When he left temporarily, there was a vacancy that nobody could fill. His return was always greeted with cries of welcome. He did not begin at the beginning, but he stayed till the end. And how he could sway his audiences ! It was this power that won for him, and Tom Stewart, the title of "tail enders." Where there were local speakers, prosy and too precise, or where there was only room for three speeches, Orlady usually closed. Why? Because his wit and eloquence and epigrammatic truths sent the audience away in high good humor. At the Oil City meeting, at the great Charleroi gathering, and in the Academy at Philadelphia, everywhere, he charmed his audience with the witchery of his tongue.

That Charleroi meeting gave the major his only opportunity to kick. And it was a quiet, but vigorous one; part of the secret history of the campaign. The expression in his great speech that day about the South raising "cotton, niggers and hell" was the occasion; it was aggravated by some ignorant colored politician trying to make capital out of a misuse of the words.

Major Orlady in that, as well as in other addresses, where he used the words, used them as a paraphrase. He compared the North with the South; the freedom of speech and ballot here, with oppression and intimidation down there, and then continuing said that the popular impression of the South was that they raised nothing but the three articles named.

"And to think that a lot of ignoramuses should raise a row about an expression that originated way back in Horace Greeley's time," he would say.

Two things that Orlady never has grown used to, and never will, are political and newspaper liars. In this instance he ran up against both.

In aptness of epigrammatic truth and beauty of expression, nothing can surpass these fragments from Major Orlady's speeches :

The home of the toiler is the corner-stone of our system ; and the man who has no home and don't want one, who has no wife and don't want one is as worthless as a tramp stealing a ride on an emigrant train.

When the morning of November 7 has come let Pennsylvania's salutation to timid capital and sullen labor be gloriously encouraging, that smokeless stacks will soon again be lurid torches ; that empty sails will soon again blow full over-weighted hulls ; that mine and mill, farm and city, man and money, will soon again unite in glad acclaim that the Republican theory is not an experiment and the chorus of a happy people will join in the benediction of the Judean shepherds, " Peace on earth and good-will to men," and that the government of the people, for the people and by the people shall not pass from earth.

The argument of the free trader stops only at assuring us of a reduction of temperature in the place of eternal torment.

The laborer here is the intelligent peer of his employer.

I care not what the dreamer and theorist may claim, I am cold-blooded enough to want results. The blazing furnace means more than the logic of the schools. A busy mill, mine or factory proves more than all the algebra of Yale or Harvard. A line of sweating laborers is more convincing than a row of logarithms.

Patriotism must supply the place of universal brotherhood. The Czar only cares for Russia, Bismarck for Germany, and Gladstone for English interests. We must run this Yankee Government of ours for our own wives and babies, and not for foreign capitalists.

I am opposed to that philanthropy which sends a box of flannel to China and permits a child around the corner to die for want of healthy food.

Free trade is a science based on assumptions. It is the theory of the millennium.

Five genii should watch the making of the ballot:—he of the yardstick, the pound weight, the dollar, the day's wages and the home.

The American laborer will not be satisfied with the black loaf of the Russian peasant, the macaroni roll of Italy. His home must not be the comfortless thatch of the European toiler. The dollar he demands for toil must not be of depreciated currency. He demands as his right, the well-heated, well-lighted, bright, airy home, where his wife and children enjoy the blessings of education, Christianity and domestic comfort, representing his investment from money that needs no resumption and will allow no repudiation.

No sentiment taken from a Democratic national platform is patriotic enough for a headline in the copy books of our common schools.

The Republican party does not believe in cheap anything, men, homes or wages. It believes in luxury rather than want, indulgence rather than hunger.

Review of the Republican record has never brought to a single adherent shame of his advocacy, or regret for its accomplishments.

Each voter this year has had an individual experience of the "before and after" using effects of Clevelandism.

Lower advalorems have given us plenty of well-clad tramps, sad-eyed women and empty pockets.

All America first, the rest of mankind second, may be national selfishness; but of the two I am for those of our own household.

I see more Americanism, more patriotism, more Pennsylvanianism in McKinleyism than I do in Wilsonism.

Capital never strikes. The dollar is a senseless thing, it don't wear clothes or sweat. Labor eats meat and must have a roof. When the dollar stops, labor wants.

CHARLES EMORY SMITH'S advent in the campaign as a spellbinder was the—to him—unconsciously dramatic event of the tour. He had just returned from Europe. He had come over in the same steamer with William L. Wilson, and with a copy of the London *Times* containing Wilson's famous London Chamber of Commerce and Free Trade speech, in his inside pocket.

HON. CHARLES EMORY SMITH.

When the editor of the Philadelphia *Press* and ex-Minister to Russia, in tightly-buttoned Prince Albert coat, stepped out in front of the magnificent audience of 4000 people in Carnegie Music Hall, Allegheny, with the great organ looming up behind him, and shook the creases out of his copy of the London *Times*, and said :

" Here is the original publication, whose correctness Mr. Wilson cannot deny," the audience cheered and laughed and cheered again, till the pipes of the big organ seemed to tremble.

The politics of the great campaign that meant something more than State convention work, and moulding of public opinion ; that involved the mingling with the great mass of the people ; with men of all colors and conditions of breath and raiment, was a trifle new to the editor-statesman. But it was also decidedly novel. One day on the train, after a particularly voluble patriot in Luzerne County had finished a half hour's face-to-face talk with the ex-minister, in which the stranger had discussed everything from the price of cow meat on the hoof up to his plans for remodeling the State government, Mr. Smith turned to one of his traveling companions with a laugh, and said :

" Look here ! Do you know that a month with this party is as good as a liberal education to any man."

Charles Emory Smith, while yet a young man, stepped into the full blaze of publicity through the mediumship of two dozen words spoken in a great political crisis. It was at the New York State Convention of 1876. The friends of Senator Conkling were demanding that his name be presented as the choice of New York for the Presidency. George William Curtis, with his followers, was on the floor endeavoring to prevent such action. Curtis had exerted all the powers of eloquent persuasion in a masterful address on the right of free speech, in which he charged the friends of Conkling with a desire to strangle the voice of his faction.

The convention was in a tumult. Curtis and his followers seemed about to triumph. The tide was setting against Conkling's hopes, when a young man near the middle of the Convention Hall rose in response to a hurried message from Conkling and Platt, who were seated upon the wide platform. He advanced to the front, where other men had stood who had tried unsuccessfully to reply to the persuasive logic of Curtis. His first words brought a hush over the clamor and turmoil.

"Mr. Chairman! We are here fighting over a mere shadow. There can be no issue of Free Speech in a free Republican convention."

There was a cheer from the Conkling followers, then more cheers as the speaker went on in his impromptu address, and at its end the decisive vote swept Conkling's name unchallenged into the place of honor which he had coveted.

At every State convention during the years that Charles Emory Smith lived and labored in New York he was made Chairman of the Committee on Resolutions. His appearance in a convention hall invariably brought forth the remark :
" Here comes Smith and the platform."

The barest outlines of a life that has been devoted to the service of the public and his party read something like this :

Born in Connecticut. Raised in Albany, N. Y. Edited a daily paper for six months when sixteen years of age, between academic and collegiate course. Taught in Albany Academy for a time. Became chief editor of Albany *Express* when twenty-three years old. Soon after became chief editor of Albany *Journal*, Thurlow Weed's old paper, and remained such until he came to the editorship of the *Press* in 1880. Delegate to National Convention of 1876, and wrote large part of platform. Delegate to every Republican State Convention of New York from 1875 to 1880, and always chairman of Committee on Platform. Minister to Russia in 1890.

Here are some gems from Mr. Smith's campaign speeches :

We are told that the Gorman Bill which passed is far better and safer than the Wilson Bill, for which it was substituted. When Parliament was alarmed by the stories of the gunpowder plot, it sent a commissioner to examine the walls of the Parliament Houses. This sapient commissioner reported that he had found seventy-five barrels of gunpowder carefully concealed beneath bundles of fagots ; that he had removed twenty-five of these barrels, and he hoped the other fifty wouldn't do any harm. Just so the champions of the Gorman Bill tell us that the Wilson Bill contained seventy-five barrels, not of gunpowder, but of dynamite to blow up American industries ; that by the Gorman Bill they had removed twenty-five of these barrels and they hoped the other fifty wouldn't do any harm. The choice between these two measures is very much like that which the good colored parson laid before his congregation, when he said :

"Men and brethren, there are only two ways open before you ; one of these ways is the broad and narrow way which leads to perdition, and the other is the straight and crooked way that leads to damnation."

In the month of May, 1889, the teeming valley of the Conemaugh was brilliant and happy with prosperity and advancement. The morning sun shed its glory on the verdant hillsides ; the blazing fires leaped from the tall chimneys ; the music of the humming machinery swelled into a diapason of joy and the people were busily employed, well-paid, contented at their toil, happy in their homes and looking forward with hope and assurance from a grateful present to a glorious future. Suddenly, the clouds gathered, the sky became black, the storm broke loose and down through the valley swept the wild torrent, carrying havoc, destruction and death upon its tumultuous bosom.

In 1892 our country stood at the very summit of prosperity and happiness. Never was the prospect so bright ; never employment so secure ; never wages so high, never our flag so greatly respected at home and abroad. The sun as it spanned the great arch of the Republic and sank every twenty-four hours beneath the golden tinted bosom of the Pacific, saw this country three million dollars richer than it was the day before. The American people were making and saving more than a thousand millions of dollars a year. Never in all history was there such a magnificent sunburst of prosperity and progress as during that memorable year. Suddenly, the storm gathered and broke loose, and, as in the Conemaugh Valley, it swept over the country and in almost the twinkling of an eye, the greatest prosperity we had ever enjoyed was succeeded by the greatest depression which the country has ever witnessed.

In 1889, it was a gallant chieftain of Pennsylvania who rushed to the rescue of the stricken people upon whom disaster had fallen in the Conemaugh Valley and who led them in the great struggle of recovery and recuperation; and in 1894 it is the same gallant son of Pennsylvania who is summoned by the people to lead them in doing their part toward the re-establishment of that policy which will rescue the country from its blighting depression. It was General Daniel H. Hastings who was your leader in 1889, and it is fitly and naturally General Daniel H. Hastings who is your leader in 1894.

When William L. Wilson declared to the London Chamber of Commerce that his bill was the beginning of a revolution which would overthrow protection in the United States, his audience, as indicated in the report in the London *Times*, broke out in exclamations of "Hear, hear!" No wonder these British manufacturers and merchants shouted "Hear, hear!" for not in a generation have they heard anything so welcome to their ears. But there are other people who will hear, hear! The American people will hear, hear! and they will also heed, heed! There is another individual who will also hear something, and if his ears are close to the ground to-night he can already hear the advance notes of that doom which was foreshadowed in the solemn hymn of good old Doctor Watts:

"Hark, from the tombs a doleful sound,
  My ears attend the cry,
Come, Billy Wilson, view the ground
  Where you must shortly lie."

I can imagine the feelings of my Democratic friends as they read the extraordinary utterances of Mr. Wilson. I am sure they felt like saying in the language of the poet, Pryor:

"Be to his virtues very kind,
Be to his faults a little blind,
Let all his ways be unconfined,
But clap a padlock on his mind."

There are great figures and great epochs in history. There are great figures like William of Orange and Cromwell and Washington and Lincoln that move along the highway of history with the tongue of inspiration and with the sword of command. Their flaming torch blazes the pathway of destiny and their lofty fellowship enkindles and ennobles the mind. As we tread the stately corridors of the centuries under their guidance, with the wide illumination of human experience and with the high motive of great achievement, new vistas open before our enraptured minds, and we feel the quickening glow of the masters. We have had a few such great epochs and new departures in our national history. When Thomas Jefferson completed the Louisiana purchase he opened the new epoch of territorial expansion beyond the Mississippi. When James Monroe and John Quincy

Adams proclaimed the Monroe doctrine they opened the new epoch of political independence of Europe. When Abraham Lincoln declared that this Republic could not live half free and half slave he marked the new epoch of the national conscience and national liberty. And so when James G. Blaine and Benjamin Harrison put into the third article of the McKinley Bill these principles, viz., a protective tariff for the defence of American labor on all foreign goods that come in competition with our own; free admission to our markets for the necessaries of life which we do not make or produce ourselves; but fair trade is fair play, and when we freely open our markets to the products of other nations they must in turn open their markets to us under reciprocal interests and arrangements. I say that when James G. Blaine and Benjamin Harrison put these principles into the McKinley Bill they opened the new epoch and marked the new departure of industrial development and commercial expansion under the two great twin Republican, American principles of protection and reciprocity.

FROM start to finish, from the first crash of dynamite cartridges in noisy welcome up at Emporium, down to the last careering Roman candle ball on the night of November 5, two men were the almost constant companions of General Hastings and General Latta during the campaign tour. They were Hon. Charles F. Warwick, City Solicitor of Philadelphia, and Hon. Henry Hall, of Pittsburg.

Hon. Charles F. Warwick.

Take Warwick first. Medium height, full, florid face and dark moustache ; high forehead, thin hair, nervous, an orator, fiery of speech, intensely practical, yet with a breadth of mind that could—and did—discuss within the limits of a quarter of an hour and with absolute accuracy as to time, place and names, the main points in Assyrian archæological research, and the early history of civilization beyond the Mississippi. A Philadelphian, happy in his home life, engrossed in his profession, a campaigner from pure love of it, and the most charming conversationalist one could meet in a month.

His keen sense of the ridiculous made Charles F. Warwick one of the central figures in every episode of any moment on the trip. As an orator he carried his audience with him.

Charles F. Warwick, City Solicitor of Philadelphia, read law in the office of E. Spencer Miller, Esq., entered the Law Department of the University of Pennsylvania, and was admitted to practice in 1873. He early took an active interest in public affairs. In 1875, when General Hartranft was a candidate for Gubernatorial honors, he was requested by the State Committee to take the stump. This was his introduction as a public political speaker. In the Garfield campaign he was sent to Ohio and Indiana, and personally accompanied Mr. Blaine through a portion of that campaign, and spoke with him on the same stump. When George S. Graham was elected District Attorney, Mr. Warwick was made one of his assistants. In 1884 he was nominated to the office of City Solicitor, and after one of the hardest political battles ever waged in this city he was elected by a majority of 14,000, running 5000 ahead of his ticket. He was re-elected to the same office in 1887 by a majority of 38,000. While in office he has argued some of the most important questions that have come before the courts, in relation to municipal law, and has successfully tried a number of very important cases. He gave an opinion in relation to five cent fare question, argued the matter, and ultimately won the case. He obtained a verdict in the " Brown " case, arising out of the case of the Gas Trust equity suit. He gave several opinions in relation to the liability of the railway companies to pave the streets from curb to curb, and, after years of litigation in the lower courts and in the Supreme Court, won the case. The result of this litigation has been the saving of at least $12,000,000 to the city and street improvements in the way of paving, that have made Philadelphia second to no city in the Union, perhaps in the world. He has interpreted, in opinions, nearly every line of the Bullitt Bill, and his opinions in no instance, have been overruled by the courts.

The following telling paragraphs are from some of Mr. Warwick's campaign utterances :

We are not 5 per cent of the entire population of the earth, yet we manufacture one-third of all the products of the earth and consume about 95 per cent of all we manufacture. We are the best clad, the best housed and the best fed people on the earth. Our market is the greatest in the world. No wonder England is anxious to control it ; no wonder she welcomed and banquetted Mr. Wilson at the Chamber of Commerce in London ; no wonder she did honor to the man who fathered the bill in the American Congress that resulted in starting the mills in Lancashire, Yorkshire and Wales, and closing those in America.

The Democratic party is a party of negation. It is like a brake on a stage coach, which may be of use in going down, but is only an additional weight in going up hill, or traveling on the level.

The difference between the "Wilson Bill" and the "McKinley Bill" is, that the former protects the industries of the Old World, the latter those of the New.

The Democratic party seems to be forever promising prosperity, but under its rule the country never catches up to the promises.

The trouble with the Democratic party is that it seems to measure prosperity by the cheapness of goods. Under its system of political economy it neglects to provide means that will enable the people to earn money that they may buy goods. The party seems to be satisfied if prices be cheap. It takes it for granted that the country is prosperous if it can point to a pair of trousers in a shop window marked one dollar. It judges prosperity by the price of goods; whether home labor goes half clad or naked, if goods be cheap, it does not seem to matter by whom they are made; where they are made or how they are made. Let me add that goods may be too cheap; low prices may mean starvation wages; may mean the loss of dignity of labor; may mean the misery and starvation of the wage-earner; may mean the cold and cheerless garret, where the sewing girl sits

> "In poverty, hunger and dirt,
> Sewing at once, with a double thread,
> A shroud, as well as a shirt."

The promises and prophecies of the Democratic party are contradicted by the conditions which surround us to-day. Their eloquent promises have vanished; their oratorical predictions have passed away like the wind; the smokeless chimneys of the mills; the dead ashes on the forge; the silence of the anvil, the spindle and the loom, give a sad and forceful answer to their specious promises of two years ago.

HARRY HALL. The name is that of one of the best fellows in the world; of an orator, a journalist, a gentleman. Not to know Harry Hall is to have lost the benefit of a broad education. Only one other man in the State of Pennsylvania can tell a story like Hall, and that is Colonel Tom Stewart. No other man in the State can talk to an audience as he can talk. The fiery vigor of his exhortations to political repentance; the rich "far-down" brogue of his

Milesian metaphors, and the religious unction of one of his Covenanter or Blue-Stocking Presbyterian stories with the scene located somewhere in Mercer County, linger in memory like the taste of a ripe peach in the mouth.

Hon. Harry Hall is a self-made man. Through vicissitude and trial he has made for himself, unaided, a name. All honor to him. He has been coal miner, school teacher, editor, member of the Legislature, lecturer. He is young yet, on the better side of forty, for all his gray hairs. He has never married; maybe it is because, with his loyalty of love, there is no place in his heart for wife and mother at the same time—and mother comes first. In the great campaign of 1894 his name is inseparably associated with its great results.

He is a native of England, but his parents emigrated to this country when he was but a baby. He has been an Abolitionist and a Republican all his life, like his father before him. "They used the Weekly New York *Tribune* as a blanket for my cradle," he jokingly remarked once.

Henry Hall worked in a coal mine till 1875, then he taught school. From this on up to the present his career in brief is as follows:

In 1878, Recorder of Mercer County. 1881, editor and part owner of the Mercer *Dispatch*. 1886, elected to the Legislature. 1888, re-elected, and was made chairman of

HON. HENRY HALL.

the Judiciary General Committee of the House. Since 1891 connected with the Pittsburg *Dispatch* and Pittsburg *Times*—now with the latter—as Legislative correspondent, special writer and Washington correspondent. Mr. Hall is a member of the Mercer Bar, having studied in the office of the present President Judge of that district, Hon. S. H. Miller, being admitted in 1886. He was at one time a member of the editorial staff of the Pittsburg *Commercial Gazette*, and during 1894 represented the Pittsburg *Times* in Washington. Mr. Hall made his first political speech in the Garfield campaign of 1880, and since then has taken part in every Republican general canvass in the State.

Mr. Hall is a graceful and forceful writer. He is one of the few men who can make a table of statistics read interesting in print. He is a descriptive writer of rare power, his letters from England a few years since being widely read and copied.

There are few men in any State who have so many friends as Harry Hall. Genial, kindly and sympathetic, he has a manner that wins its way to men's hearts before they are aware of it.

Some extracts from his campaign speeches follow:

Ever since I can remember the Democratic party has told the people that if they would only entrust it with power, it would right all wrongs, reform all abuses, and administer the government in the interests of the whole people. For years the people listened to these pleas and promises with unheeding ears, but in 1892 they took the

Democracy at its word and turned the government in all its branches into its hands. And now, after almost two years of sole control, what has been the result? It needs no recital from me. The people have seen it. The people know it, and know it to their sorrow.

I sometimes think that the average Democrat, as in the solitude of his own thoughts he reflects upon what his party promised and what his party has done, must feel as the old Scotch-Irishman felt when he prayed thus: "Oh, Lord, Thou has left us to the freedom of our own will, and a fine fist we have made of it."

They have kept no promise, they have fulfilled no pledge. Promising everybody everything, to get into power, they have been unable when in power to do anything, because they could not agree upon anything. Discordant in everything but the desire for power, they have been discordant in all their attempts to fulfill their pledges and on the tariff, the silver question, the State banks question, and our foreign relations—upon every issue, they have made an utter and lamentable failure. They have been weighed in the balance and found wanting. The people know it. The Democrats know it themselves.

And now what shall we do? There is but one way, and that is for every man, not as a Republican, not as a Democrat, but as a citizen interested in his country's best and truest interests, to endeavor to undo the evils that are weighing down our industries and our people. It is a plain way, a straight way. Vote the straight Republican ticket. Democrats, come with us and we will do you good. Why will you stay over there feeding upon the dry, dead husks of Democracy, when in your Republican father's house there is bread enough and to spare?

Come with us and we will put a new robe upon you. It is a white robe, it is a clean robe. No stain of slavery, secession or treason mars its whiteness. We will write a new name upon your forehead. It is a glorious name. Abraham Lincoln bore it. Ulysses S. Grant bore it. James A. Garfield bore it. James G. Blaine bore it. That rugged rock of Republicanism, "Tom" Reed, of Maine, bears it. That man whose name is loved wherever a workingman swings a hammer or a pick, wherever a wheel turns or a spindle hums, William McKinley, of Ohio, bears it. Ten thousand memories cluster around that name—patriotic memories, tender and loving memories, glorious memories, immortal memories, all cluster around that name, REPUBLICAN.

Sometimes, during the past eighteen months, when I have seen all the business paralyzation, the smokeless factories and mills, the closed mines, the idle men, and women and children in poverty and want, I have said to myself, "Why should we Republicans have to bear this? We did not vote for this change. Why should not its effects fall alone upon those who voted for it?" I felt a little like the Irishman who went into a restaurant and asked for something to eat. A plate of food was set before him. He looked at it and asked:

"What's that?"

"Hash."

"Hash, is it?" he said. "Well, begorra, lave the man who chawed it ate it."

Now that is the way I sometimes feel with regard to our present troubles—"lave them who chawed it ate it." But that can't be done. The good or the evil effects of all our laws fall upon all the people alike. If a law is good for a Republican it is good for a Democrat. If it is bad for a Democrat it is bad for a Republican. And we all have a privilege in common. If we make a change and don't like it, we can change back again. The great court of the people is always open, and there is always the right of appeal at the next election from what does not suit us in the results of the last. Let us take an appeal from the results of 1892 to the court of the people, held at the polls in November, 1894.

Now it is certain that Daniel H. Hastings will be elected Governor of Pennsylvania, and elected by the largest majority ever given a Gubernatorial candidate in the United States. But do you know how it will be done? I'll tell you. By every Republican, by every Democrat dissatisfied with the present condition of affairs, going early to the polls on election day and voting the straight Republican ticket.

A hundred years or more ago, when there were savage Indians on the frontiers of Western Pennsylvania, an old Presbyterian minister was preparing one Sabbath morning to go out and preach to his scattered flock. One of his elders came to accompany him, and found the minister loading his old musket with a ball and four slugs.

"Ah, Brother McCracken," says he, "I fear you are depending upon the arm of the flesh. If it is foreordained that an Indian is to kill you this morning, what earthly hand can stay the blow?"

"That's all right, Brother McElroy," said the minister, ramming home the charge, "that's all right. But if, on the other hand, it is foreordained that I'm to kill an Indian this morning, I'll do it the quicker if I have my gun with me."

Now it may be foreordained that Hastings is to be elected by a big majority, but the way to make sure of it is for every man to go to the polls on election day and vote the straight Republican ticket.

MARIOTT BROSIUS possesses that peculiar power which holds an audience to the sway of his eloquence. The words, not so much the manner, of the man have given him the reputation of an orator which he so well deserves. Judged by the superficial standard of gesticulation, voice and mobility of feature, he is not an orator: judged by his language, his eloquence and wit place him in the front rank. And this is the secret of his power. It is this that has carried him into great campaigns outside the State and made him a name in other commonwealths, as a speaker, and in congress as a debater.

He is a young man yet, this Congressman from the famous Lancaster district, only fifty-two. He was a farmer's boy, of Quaker stock, who got his education in the country schools and at Chestnut Hill Academy. He was a soldier in the Ninety-seventh Pennsylvania Infantry, and at the front when he was eighteen. While nobly trying to help a wounded comrade he was

wounded at Bermuda Hundred, and from that day to this he has never raised one arm. He was commissioned a lieutenant, and mustered out in '65. He graduated from the University of Michigan in 1868, and was admitted to the bar the same year. He was a candidate for Congressman-at-large in 1882, but was defeated, though he ran 7200 votes ahead of his ticket. He was elected to Congress in 1888, and to every term since. He is an LL. D. of Ursinus College.

In personal appearance Mr. Brosius is tall, with dignified mien, and well-poised head. He wears a full beard, and moustache, and would be taken for a Presbyterian clergyman were he not so well known as a Congressman.

Here are some of his choicest utterances in the Great campaign :

> The circumstances of the Democratic party, inward and outward, present to the compassionate mind every claim to sympathy and commiseration. Their situation calls to mind an observation of Thomas H. Benton concerning John C. Calhoun. These distinguished Democrats loved each other with the same intense devotion as David B. Hill and Grover Cleveland. After the death of Calhoun a friend asked Benton what he had to say about Calhoun. He replied, " Nothing at all, sir. When the Almighty puts His hands on a man I take mine off."

There are two periods in human life in which a person is not expected to do a man's work: the feebleness of childhood and the decrepitude of age. Great exertions cannot be expected from either cradles or crutches. The Democratic party is on crutches.

The soup house, the vagrant, the industrial tramp have been the distinguishing characteristics, the badge and insignia of the Cleveland régime.

A Democratic minister was once called in to open the session of a Democratic House in the absence of the Chaplain. He prayed with great unction and power. This was a portion of his invocation: "We pray Thee, O Lord, to guard and protect the members of this House. each and every one of them. Keep them as far from sin and wrong, O Lord, as Thou art *from them.*"

I cannot contemplate with patience the statement of a Democratic paper that the President did well to slap in the face the "dirty beggars" called pensioners. Such a man can well be dismissed with the tribute paid to another, in a similar case, by a distinguished American: "If he had been born a bird he would have been a buzzard; if he had been born a beast he would have been a panther; if he had been born a fish he would have been a mud-cat; if he had been born a reptile he would have been a lizard; if he had been born an insect he would have been a bed-bug."

No other policy of our government can shed upon our history so fadeless a lustre as our liberality toward the defenders of the Union. When the muse of history shall record the achievements and recite the glories of the republic, she will put for American Patriotism the overthrow of treason and rebellion and the restoration of the Union. For American Heroism she will write of the unrivaled splendor of the martial valor exhibited on the battlefields of the Union, North and South. For the Charity of the republic she will write in figures of gold the fabulous sums disbursed to assuage distress, relieve suffering and dispense the consolations of religion in the dark night of war. For the Magnanimity of the nation she will point with pride to the parole of a vanquished army and amnesty to every American citizen who bore arms against his country. Then dipping her pen in the sunlight she will write on the clear blue high above them all, for God and the angels to read, the enormous sums carried on the pension rolls of the nation to stand for the republic's imperishable gratitude to her heroic defenders.

ONE day away back in the winter of 1856 a devoted Sunday school teacher in the English Lutheran Church in Altoona, who was interested in the temporal as well as the spiritual welfare of his scholars, rapped at the door of a modest home in that growing city, and inquired for one of his boys, named George. He wanted him to go to work in the finishing department of the Pennsylvania Railroad shops, and help out for a few weeks, as there was a rush of work on just then. The lad, then fourteen, went to work the next morning, and from that day dated the rise of George Franklin Huff, ex-State Senator, and to-day one of the two congressmen-at-large from the superb commonwealth of Pennsylvania.

A year or so later, young Huff became regularly apprenticed as a car finisher, and it is one of the striking points in his life that in all the subsequent years he never had but two employers, the Pennsylvania Railroad Company and W. M. Lloyd & Co., bankers. At the time that this lad, with his veins throbbing with the sturdy blood of Pennsylvania Dutch ancestors for four generations, was learning his trade, Frank Thomson, now second vice-president of the Pennsylvania, was learning his trade in the machine shops; Robert Pitcairn, superintendent of the Pittsburg Division, was a telegrapher in the Altoona office, and Andrew Carnegie was assistant to the superintendent of the Pittsburg Division, Col. Thomas Scott, afterward president.

It was through the latter that George F. Huff rose. A young man was occasionally needed to keep a sharp eye on the vault where the money for the payment of the men in the shops was deposited, and young Huff was called in from the shop and assigned to this task. The manner of the young man attracted Mr. Scott's attention, and he recommended him to the banking firm of W. M. Lloyd & Co., as a desirable person for the position of clerk in their employ. To Mr. Huff was assigned the work of looking after the pay-cash of the Pennsylvania Railroad. The young mechanic was equal to the emergency. He did his work to such complete satisfaction of his employers

Hon. George F. Huff,
Congressman-at-Large.

that in a few years he was taken into the firm and sent to Greensburg to establish a branch bank and take complete control of it.

During the early years of his connection with W. M. Lloyd & Co., it was part of Mr. Huff's duty to carry the Pennsylvania Railroad pay-money from Philadelphia to Altoona. This frequently amounted to $60,000 in cash. Yet he never lost a dollar.

He remained with Lloyd & Co. for years, until their financial stringency in the seventies compelled a severance of business relations. Since then he has been in business for himself as banker, coal operator and capitalist. He has a beautiful home in Greensburg, where he has entertained many distinguished men, among them President Harrison, and where during the late campaign, on two memorable occasions, he entertained General Hastings and the members of his party, together with Robert Pitcairn, C. L. Magee, Judge John Gripp, George M. Von Bon-horst and others, with a hospitality that cannot be forgotten.

Few men know it, for he never refers to the matter for political or other effect, but Hon. Geo. F. Huff holds an honorable discharge from the Union army. His parents refused to permit him to enlist, but one day the war music grew so loud in his ears that it drowned all parental commands, and that day he went off in a uniform of blue, beating time on his drum for the march of Pennsylvania volunteers.

Congressman Huff is of medium height, of stout build, affable manner, kindly of heart, benevolent, and impulsive for good. He is one of the most generally admired men in Western Pennsylvania, because of his elevation of character and kindliness of disposition. He is a worker rather than a speaker. In public speech he is plain, straightforward, business-like, as these brief extracts from his address as presiding officer at the great Greensburg meeting indicate :

> I deem it a high honor to be called upon to preside at a meeting such as this. This great demonstration following the monster meeting held at Jeannette this afternoon, indicates to my mind very clearly that the voters of Westmoreland County will at the approaching election contribute their full share of the influence necessary to a speedy resumption of business.

> I have recently met many persons who have heretofore acted with our political opponents, who declare most positively they will support the Republican candidates this fall. They know why wages have been reduced; they also know why it is difficult to procure any kind of employment at any fair wages.

> I am quite sure the people of this county, irrespective of previous party affiliation, will aid us in our efforts to

restore business prosperity and to revive the drooping industries of the country. A healthy system which will protect all American products is our only shield against foreign encroachment. I very much mistake the present temper of our people if they have not concluded to again place their interests in the keeping of the Republican party.

ELEVEN o'clock at night. An opera house with its stage and balconies draped with flags and banners, packed to its capacity. Men and women standing in the aisles to the orchestra rail. Wearied through pure physical strain of sitting and standing for four long hours, enraptured with the wit and eloquence and logic of Hastings, and Charles Emory Smith, Orlady, Latta and Warren, yet waiting to hear somebody else, the crowd showed no desire to vacate the building. Occasionally at the close of some speech, there would arise a spasmodic cry for this one man. When all courtesy had been extended to the speakers from a distance, and to the candidates, a yell went up from every part of the building. It voiced but one word, and the burden of the cry was:

"Stone! Stone! Charlie Stone! Speech! speech!"

This incident of the great Oil City meeting is but one of the many which indicate the esteem and admiration in which Hon. Charles Warren Stone, ex-Lieutenant Governor of Pennsylvania, ex-Secretary of the Commonwealth, and the present Congressman from the Twenty-seventh District, is held by his constituents and the people among whom he has spent all the years of his mature life.

HON. CHARLES W. STONE.

It would require the limits of a small volume to record the public services of Congressman Stone. His career has been distinguished by its uprightness, its freedom from reproach and its eminent success under all circumstances. Charles W. Stone was born in 1843, the son of a member of the Legislature of Massachusetts. He is of Revolutionary ancestry, was a farmer's lad, then a school teacher, and finally, by his unaided effort, put himself through Williams College and graduated with high honors. When he was barely of age he came to Warren, Pa., as principal of its public school. From this on his public life has been as follows :

In 1869 he was elected to the House of Representatives and was returned in 1870. In 1876 he was elected to the State Senate, and in 1878 was nominated Lieutenant Governor on the same ticket with General Henry M. Hoyt, who was the nominee for Governor, and elected. In 1887 he was appointed Secretary of the Commonwealth, and in 1890 was nominated and elected to Congress in the district which he now represents.

In personal appearance the Ex-Lieutenant-Governor is of medium height, rather slender, with dark hair, eyes, and full beard. He speaks slowly but with great force and decision. He attempts no oratorical outbursts ; his clear cut logic appeals to the reason of his hearers without the aid of carefully rounded periods as the grace-notes of poetry. Unfortunately Ex-Lieutenant-Governor Stone speaks without notes and so the chronicler of these records has to forego the pleasure of presenting extracts from Mr. Stone's numerous addresses during the campaign of 1894.

A YOUNG man with clear-cut features and an upright military carriage, was greeted down in the Beaver Valley by the spellbinders as "Everett ;" frequently as "Warren," and oftenest as "Major." He was tall and slender, with premature gray threads in his black hair, dark eyes that looked at the world through plain eye-glasses, a dark moustache and a winning way. This was Major Everett Warren, president of the State League of Republican Clubs of Pennsylvania. He had come on from Scranton to help inspire the people of Western Pennsylvania, and especially the young men, with some of the Republican fervor that burned in his own blood.

Major Warren is one of the most conspicuous members of the Lackawanna bar. He is wealthy and his wealth has been acquired by his own untiring industry in his profession. Better than all, however, Everett Warren is a man of the people. There is no false pride in his make-up. He began life as a newsboy in his native city. Then he became a cash boy in a store, then a clerk in a law office. What he is he has made himself. He was not ashamed to wheel his own trunk to the depot when he began his university career at Yale because he would not go in debt to somebody else to do it for him.

Major Warren's military title is derived through active and honorable membership in the Pennsylvania National

MAJOR EVERETT WARREN

Guard. In 1881 he enlisted as a private in A Company of the crack Thirteenth Regiment, under Captain, now Lieutenant Governor, Louis A. Watres. After three years' service in the ranks, Private Warren became sergeant-major, then adjutant and finally judge advocate of the Third brigade, with the rank of major on General J. P. S. Gobin's staff. After a continuous service of over ten years, Major Warren resigned as judge advocate in 1891 and withdrew from the guard.

Here are some of the bright things he said during the ten days he spent with the Hastings party:

The grand old party, and no sneers can detract one iota from its well-earned name or its great achievements, has sounded the bugle that shall never signal retreat. We are going to get back again all our flags and cannon. Let us buckle on our armor and march together like the Macedonian Phalanx of old, with locked shields and measured tread. "Protection to American labor and capital; protection to American money; protection to American ballots; honest men for office," are the mottoes that shine down on us from the Republican banner, while over it hover the eagles of victory.

I met an employe of the largest single industry of Northeastern Pennsylvania, the Bessemer rail mills of the Lackawanna Iron and Steel Company, the other day, on his way to his mid-day meal. He stopped, and, pointing to a large patch on his knee asked me if I knew what that was.

"Of course I do; that is a patch!"

"Oh no," he answered; "that is not a patch."

"What do you call it then?" I asked.

"Why the fellows down in the mill call it a Democratic badge."

Two years ago the people were misled by a lot of office-seeking demagogues, professional calamity howlers and political rain makers, into deserting the party of law, liberty and progress. And then the trouble began. They were like the man who, while breaking a yoke of steers held by a rope, having occasion to use both his hands in letting down a pair of bars, fetched the rope around one of his legs. That instant something frightened the steers and the unfortunate farmer was snaked off his feet on a wild, erratic excursion a mile or so over rough ground, as long as the rope lasted. His neighbors gathered him up and waited around for him to come to. When he did, one of them inquired how he came to do such a foolish thing as to hitch a rope around his leg under such circumstances.

"Waal," he said, "we hadn't gone five rod afore I seen my mistake."

The situation of the Democratic party just now is exactly like that of the little Arkansas boy whom a gentleman met on his way to school with his pail in his hand. Tapping the urchin on the head, the gentleman kindly inquired:

"Well, my son, I suppose you learn to read at school?"

"No, sir."

"What, not learn to read? Then you learn to spell?"

"No, sir."

"Not learn to spell? Do you count?"

"No, sir."

"My boy, what do you do?"

"Wait for school to let out." The Democrats are just waiting for the election to come off. They are not making any campaign.

LOOKING back through a stretch of twenty-five years there comes to the memory of the writer a tall, slender, retiring young man, who came quietly and sat in a rear seat in a literary society connected with the Washington Public Schools of Pittsburg. He rarely took an active part in the exercises, literary or parliamentary. He was from "across the river;" over in Millvale, as it was then called. The tall, slender, retiring young man of 1870, is to-day the tall, slender, dignified, gray-haired Lieutenant-Governor-elect, Hon. Walter Lyon, of Allegheny.

The keeper of the campaign records has little to say about the performances of the second on the ticket on the stump last fall. The same quiet reserve; a disinclination to attract public attention to himself or his achievements, is a characteristic of Walter Lyon to-day as it was a quarter of a century ago when he was a school teacher over in Shaler township, opposite Pittsburg. But people who know him; who possess his confidence, or friendship, see him as others do not. Affability, jollity, good-fellowship and a sturdy faithfulness to friends in Mr. Lyon are component parts of his make-up—but he does not wear them where the world may always see them and criticise with compliment or condemnation. Mr. Lyon has made his way by the exercise of none of the arts of the politician or the "patter" of the demagogue. That is why some care-hardened

Hon. Walter Lyon,
Lieutenant-Governor.

politicians wonder at his success. But he has been a success—will be a success.

There is not much to tell about his life. Here it is as he wrote it,—all legislators have to write their biographies for Smull's, bear that in mind— for the Legislative Handbook :

Walter Lyon, Allegheny County, was born in Shaler Township, Allegheny County, Pa., April 27, 1853; admitted to bar January, 1877, and has continued in practice ; is member of law firm of Lyon, McKee & Sanderson, of Pittsburg. Was appointed United States Attorney for western district of Pennsylvania June, 1889, and commissioned for four years from January 27, 1890, which position he resigned to accept his seat in the Senate.

That is all. No hint of early struggles, no suggestion of the vicissitudes that marked his early manhood and developed his inherent backwardness into a rugged self-reliance. His father was a real estate operator, and he gave his children a thorough education. That was Walter Lyon's legacy. It was the one talent that was not laid away in a napkin, as the world to-day knows.

COLONEL WILLIAM A. STONE, who stands to-day in the Congress of the United States as the conspicuous champion of a purer Americanism, was, for over a week, one of the spellbinders of the campaigning party. Big of body and brain, he struck sledge-hammer blows with voice and logic. It is characteristic of William A. Stone to deal in facts, and to take the shortest cut to conclusions. No attempt at anecdote, few metaphors or similes, no hyperbole, no anything but the earnest statement of political and economic truth seemed to cross his lips. It

HON. WILLIAM A. STONE.

was his tower of strength; he reached men in a way others could not. The life story of the success of this man runs about as follows:

Born Tioga County, Pa., April 18, 1846. Three other brothers, all in the Union Army. Enlisted in Company A, 187th Pennsylvania Volunteers, when not quite eighteen years of age, as a private. Promoted to corporal, sergeant, orderly, and second lieutenant. Mustered out at the close of the war. Attended Wellsborough Academy and Mansfield State Normal School, graduating in June, 1868. Taught Wellsborough Academy and studied law with Hon. S. F. Wilson and Hon. Jerome B. Niles. Admitted to the bar 1870. Lieutenant Colonel in the National Guard and District Attorney Tioga County 1873. Resigned in 1876, and moved to Pittsburg. In 1880 appointed United States District Attorney. In 1886 was removed by President Cleveland for pernicious activity in making Republican speeches. Was nominated for Congress by convention after Colonel Thomas M. Bayne's refusal to accept the nomination in 1890. A number objecting to the nomination because he had not been a candidate before the convention, he threw up the nomination, became a candidate at new primaries, was nominated and elected by a large majority. Elected again in 1892, and has just been re-elected. Is the author of the "Stone Immigration Bill," and member of the Judiciary Committee in the House.

Some of the utterances of Colonel Stone on the stump will be found in the succeeding paragraphs :

Sam Randall believed and talked for tariff for revenue only, with incidental protection. That has been the cry of the Pennsylvania Democrats for the last thirty years ; that to-day is the watchword and the battle-cry of the Republican party. We favor tariff for revenue with incidental protection, and that is where we stand and where we always stood. The Southern Democrats have changed the chart of the party; they now steer to the chart of tariff for revenue only.

The labor market of this country belongs to the men and women of this country, and the same principle of protection that keeps out imports to give labor to our own people, would extend protection to our laboring people by relieving them from competition with the cheap pauper labor of Europe.

The time has come when we should begin to legislate for our own people and our own country, rather than to encourage people of other countries to come to us.

I have no hostility to foreigners—I am willing that all who now live in this country should remain—but if they as well as we, are to be happy as well as prosperous, receiving fair compensation for our labor, we must close the gates part way at least and shut off this great flood that is annually pouring in upon us. Protection, as I understand it, should protect the laborer as well as the manufacturer, labor as well as capital.

SOMEBODY on the grand rounds after Col. B. Frank Eshleman, of Lancaster, had joined the tourists, referred to him as a "chuckle done up in cassimere." It was a delicate way of putting the jollity and amiability of a leading member of the Lancaster bar to the front. His coming, toward the end of the campaign, was one of the pleasing episodes of the tour. His personality is of a character to win friends and keep them, and in this respect he had few superiors among the campaigners.

As a speaker Colonel Eshleman is logical and forceful, preferring to deal with facts and figures rather than simile and metaphor. He is the happy possessor of the gift of repartee, which served him in good stead during the campaign.

COLONEL B. FRANK ESHLEMAN.

"Here, don't you say anything against England," yelled somebody in the crowd, while Eshleman was addressing a large meeting at Manayunk, and in the course of the tariff discussion was commenting upon a comparison of the blessings of the American wage-earner and those of the British laborer. To this he replied like a flash:

God forbid that I should say anything against Great Britain, for she has the best government on the face of the earth for her people and her institutions, and I should despise the man who comes to our shore from hence, who would not respect his nation.

But I hold that when an Englishman or Irishman comes to this country, he leaves his home as the young man leaves his parents to set up business and housekeeping for himself. Divine command has it, "Thou shalt love thy father and thy mother," and so should every foreigner honor the place of his nativity; but when he comes to America, he marries a wife, her name is Miss Columbia; he renounces father and mother, he must swear to love, honor, cherish and protect his own bride, forsaking all other ties and relations. He must learn to love our country, our institutions, our form of government, and our America must be his America. Then and then only will he be a good citizen, then and then only does he entitle himself to the blessings he enjoys here, then and then only will he denounce the "striker," the "anarchist," the man of "isms," and the enemies of a free government—one of the people, by the people, and for the people.

———

Here are some of the bright things from Col. Eshleman's speeches:

I am in favor of surrounding the United States with a fence "horse high, hog low and bull strong," against any foreign immigration that is not willing to subscribe to American conditions.

———

The foreigner who comes to these shores must realize that he is a factor in a country which has no king, queen or emperor; no princes, dukes, lords, counts and viscounts; no thrones and no dynasties, but where the humblest citizen may by his own effort and industry rise to the highest altitude and eminence in any department in life. And that by so doing his full duty in his citizenship, day by day, the blue in yonder flag will grow bluer, the red more cheery, the white purer, and the stars, so rapidly increasing in number, will grow more lustrous.

———

There is a good devout Christian lady in my county, who is a member of the Methodist Church, and is the mother of nineteen children. Her pastor, in conformity with the usages of the church, was called to labor in another Conference. Before leaving, he called upon this good old lady, and after giving her and her children a benediction, was just leaving the house, when the mother suddenly said, "Oh, parson, have you seen my last baby?" "No," said the parson, "and I never expect to."

WILLIAM I. SCHAFFER—he of the curling hair, towering form and eloquent tongue—was the youngest of the campaigners. He is young in years, but old, oh, so old, in political experience. Behind his tall form there is a background of success that has come to few of older years. This talented young member of the Delaware bar has been honored by the quiet Quakers and busy artisans of his county as no other young man—if Congressman "Jack" Robinson be excepted—has been honored. He holds their confidence and esteem. He has shown himself worthy of it, and the perfection of manhood in experience which the years must bring will see him still more greatly honored.

He is a lawyer, able, keen, and far-sighted, one of the young men who sat at the feet of that Gamaliel of Southeastern Pennsylvania, Judge Broomall. Mr. Schaffer, though barely past the quarter century mark, has filled and is filling

WILLIAM I. SCHAFFER, ESQ.,
District Attorney of Delaware County.

with distinction and ability the position of District Attorney of his county; as County Chairman he imparted a vigor to the Republican organization in Delaware that it had never known before.

As a campaign orator he has no equal for his years. At all times eloquent, with flashes of wit, and bursts of brilliant metaphor, he was one of the most popular speakers in the great campaign throughout the State.

Read some of his utterances below :

What is the reward we are to receive for breaking down the barriers which kept Great Britain out of the markets of America? Mr. William L. Wilson and his free trade friends answer, "The markets of the world." Almost 200,000 miles of railroad in this country of ours go to make up the network of civilization, which binds the pine tree State of Maine to the sunlit golden shores of the Pacific—the watery wastes of the lakes to the traffic-laden bosom of the gulf. These miles of rail are freighted with a commerce, in wealth so vast, that the mind of man can scarcely comprehend the figures that a twelvemonth makes. Upon these bands of steel spanning a continent and up and down our rivers and our lakes our trade is free with every corner of our common country.

This we propose to surrender for what—for a something that a little band of free trade theorists call the markets of the world—to give this up to England, now mistress of the marts of trade in every other clime, and having given up our vantage ground to her we are to wrest from her that which she already has. She conquered foreign trade with frowning battleships and red-coated men of war. With every other market open to her, she seeks for ours, and there are Americans, high in place and station, claiming to be of the political school of Jefferson and Jackson, England's worst enemies in the olden days, who would give her what she asks.

The common people of our land are wiser in their day and generation than the so-called leaders of Democratic thought. The people believe in America for Americans, native and foreign born. The patriotic masses in the nation rather than theorize about the markets of the world, are glad to know that in a few days there is to glide down the ways from the great shipyard of William Cramp & Son, into the river Delaware, the most splendid exhibition of man's handicraft and skill the sun shines on, a transoceanic steamer.

What can stir the pulses of Americans quicker and awaken their patriotism and pride more than to know, from the statement of her builders, that every pound of material in that queen of the seas from keel to topmast and from stem to stern, came from America! – the wood from American forests, the steel from American mines, fashioned by American brain and American brawn, that at her peak will fly the starry banner of the Republic made from American silk, woven on American looms. When for the first time she steams into the harbors of the old world, every American heart on board will beat faster as she bows on old ocean's waves to the shipping of other lands and salutes them with the message, "I am an American."

The Democratic party has neither principles, precepts nor creed in this campaign. Mr. Cleveland says Democracy means one thing, Mr. Hill that it means another, and in Pennsylvania it means still something else. Nowhere does it possess certain marks of identification. It is like the dog a philanthropic old Quaker saw for several days in succession, tied to a post in the baggage-room at

Broad Street Station ; each day it grew thinner and more woe-begone looking. The compassion of the old Quaker was touched :

"Can thee tell me whose dog that is, and where it is from and what its destination is?" asked the old Quaker of the baggage smasher.

"No," replied that worthy descendant of Samson, the temple wrecker, "I cannot tell thee whose dog it is, nor where it is from, nor where it is bound to, because the darned beast has eaten its tag."

It was once beautifully said by a world-famed orator, " The Republican party with the wand of progress touched the auction block and it became a school-house." To-day it may be said : The Democratic party with the axe of ruin struck the factory and it became a soup house.

If the great object lessons of the past eighteen months of Democratic misrule could be flashed, aurora like, above the horizon for the affrighted gaze of our people to look upon, they would gather en masse, as the ancients did to drive away an eclipse of the sun ; their place of meeting the election polls in every district, and the object of their anger and their fear the party of closed factories, silent mills, broken banks and broken pledges.

JEROME B. NILES became a campaigner with the Hastings party at DuBois shortly after the opening of the campaign. The first night out he gave evidence of his wide acquaintance through the State by taking dinner with friends, a practice which his extended friendship greatly encouraged. General Niles, with his thirty years of proud public record, was with the party in some of its most exciting episodes and under some most interesting circumstances. He was one of the three speakers at the unique Claysville meeting, and one of the ten at the midnight meeting at Coalport. His strong, persuasive voice was never used to better effect than at the Claysville meeting. Everywhere he went he met men who had voted for him for Auditor General in 1883, and who had some pleasant memories of the campaign to recall.

In personal appearance General Niles is of medium height, rather stout, with full, closely cropped gray beard, a pleasing manner and a vigorous, resonant voice. He has had a varied experience in politics in the sixty years of his life. He was admitted to the Tioga bar in 1861, and the following year was chosen message clerk of the House for 1862–64. He served as District Attorney of his county two terms, and was a member of the Constitutional Convention in 1872. He was first elected to the House of Representatives in 1869, then 1881–1883 he was returned. He was elected Auditor General in 1883, and was again chosen for the House in 1893 and 1895.

HON. JEROME B. NILES.

ALFRED J. NILES, ESQ.

IT is not often that father and son appear side by side on the same platform in a political campaign, but this was seen in October, when Jerome B. Niles and his son, Alfred J. Niles, spoke on the same day, from the same platform. Alfred J. Niles promises, in brains, energy and political ambition to be the counterpart of his father. He has clear-cut views, is logical, and expresses himself forcibly.

He was born in Wellsboro, Tioga County, Pa., on the twenty-seventh day of November, 1866. He attended the high school of Wellsboro, and was graduated in May, 1885. During the year 1885–86 he attended the Harrisburg Academy. In September, 1886, he entered the office of his father and began to read law. In September, 1887, he entered the Harvard Law School, and took the regular three years' course at that institution, and was graduated from it in June, 1890. Was admitted to the bar of Tioga County on September 5, 1890, and immediately was taken into the law firm of Jerome B. Niles & Sons. He practiced law in Wellsboro until August, 1894, when he went to Pittsburg and was admitted to the Pittsburg bar. He is now located in Pittsburg in the practice of his profession.

HON. HENRY WILBER PALMER, one of Pennsylvania's distinguished sons, who has filled with honor the high place of Attorney General of this State, joined the party at Wilkesbarre for a few days. General Palmer's vigorous personality and directness of speech made him a marked figure even among the coterie of speakers with whom General Hastings had surrounded himself. There is no subterfuge about General Palmer. His political enemies admit this. There is a directness about his manner of forcing conclusions or scoring a point that is absolutely painful to his political enemies sometimes. This same directness of purpose is traceable in every phase of his life. Some years ago he was asked for his biography for a certain publication, and this was the answer sent:

HON. HENRY WILBER PALMER

Henry Wilber Palmer. Born 1839. Admitted to bar 1861, in Luzerne County. Served in army one year. Elected to Constitutional Convention 1872. Appointed attorney general by Governor H. M. Hoyt, 1879. Since expiration of office in 1883, has practiced his profession in Wilkesbarre.

General Palmer's speeches during the campaign were like his autobiography, to the point, as the extracts on the following page will indicate.

The same courage and enterprise that made this western wilderness blossom like a rose, that spanned it with 170,000 miles of railroads, that built over it a network of telegraphs, and planted in it great hives of industry and thrift, will infuse energy and new life into the patient that has been in the hands of the Democratic doctors, and will make it live and thrive again.

But we are told that times are not so hard; that business is looking up—being on the flat of its back it cannot well look in any other direction.

"It is reviving." So it is. In nineteen months of pinching want, clothing, machinery, carpets, furniture, and wagons have worn out. They must be replaced, and factories must run to make them. People must eat, and the business of life must go on. It will revive. Even free traders and tariff reformers have not been able to kill it quite. It is reviving. The magnificent courage and energy of the American people will not let it die.

Do not despair of the republic! It is only a baby yet. Our 65,000,000 are only a fraction of the number that can be supported in peace and comfort on our soil. We have nearly one-half of the arable land of the earth, with but twenty people to the square mile, while Belgium has 450. We have a fertile soil, a healthful climate, a free government in which liberty, fraternity and equality, for which the world has striven, lo, these many years, are household words, so familiar that we almost doubt the old world tales of peoples being driven like dumb cattle by kings and priests. The great republic will go on prospering and to prosper, because the people intend this very year to send the false prophets and false teachers into everlasting, resurrectionless oblivion.

ALTHOUGH not a member of the tourist combination for more than a day through the State, yet the work done in Philadelphia, on the same stage with General Hastings and his friends, merits a place here for George S. Graham, District Attorney of Philadelphia, and LL. D. by

HON. GEORGE S. GRAHAM,
District Attorney of Philadelphia County.

the grace of Lafayette College. No one who has ever heard him speak can forget the force and eloquence of his words. It is this power to sway men's minds for justice and right, coupled with high legal attainments, that has placed George

S. Graham in the Chair of Criminal Law of the University of Pennsylvania and has given him fifteen years of consecutive service as District Attorney, three times having no opposition.

Mr. Graham is a Philadelphian, born here September 13, 1850. He was educated by tutor and in the public schools, and graduated from the Law Department of the University in 1871. In that same year he was admitted to the bar. He served three years as a member of Select Council, and resigned in 1880 to accept the District Attorneyship.

As a painter of vivid word pictures Mr. Graham has few equals on the rostrum. He maintains that it is better that a thousand unworthy men should draw pensions than that one worthy scar-worn veteran or dependent widow should suffer. In illustrating this theme at one of the great Philadelphia meetings, Mr. Graham painted this beautiful picture :

The moon piercing the fleecy clouds silvered the dewdrops on the blades of grass about the sleeping soldiers. The weary march was ended. Stretched upon the ground they slept. Exhausted nature sought restoration in deep slumber. Close by the road, no covering but the sky ; no couch but the green sward. One moves and stirs. Rising from his place with outstretched hands and eager face he moves swiftly away. On, on, he goes over hill and valley until many miles are passed and he stops in front of a little cottage in the country village where two years before he bade good-bye to wife and children and with many comrades marched to the front to defend his country's flag.

Before the gate he pauses for a moment, then gently lifting the latch moves along the path, climbs up to where a light gleams from one of the upper windows. Here a sight meets him that quickens his pulse, and calls a tear of joy to his eye. There is the wife and mother. One curly head already rests on the pillow, the other is buried in the mother's lap, while the little hands are clasped, and the muffled words of the evening prayer reach the listener without. "God bless papa," the mother speaks, and the infant lips repeat the prayer. Swiftly towards the window the listening soldier creeps. He can stand it no longer. He must embrace his treasures. When suddenly, the rattle of musketry and the shouts of men and the rude awakening of his comrades to repel the midnight assault dispel the sweet vision.

Alas, it was only a dream. Thoroughly aroused, into the deadly peril he moves, and instead of the vision of loved ones he stands face to face with determined foes; instead of the prattling prayer, he hears the rattle of musketry; instead of clasping dear ones to his heart, he meets the bayonet thrust, and suffering, wounded, mayhap dying, he lies upon the field. He has periled all for country. That country can never pay the debt she owes to her brave citizen soldiery.

(———)

A TALL, heavily built young man with a strong face was one of the tourists for a time, speaking with effect at Reading and other points. It was Linn Hartranft, of Philadelphia, son of the famous General and ex-Governor John F. Hartranft.

The paternal American ancestor of the family, Tobias Hartranft, arrived at Philadelphia on the twenty-third day of September, 1734. His mother was Sallie Douglass Sebring, still living, daughter of Judge Sebring, of Easton, Pa., and through her he comes from Revolutionary ancestors, in consequence of which he is a member of the Sons of the Revolution.

He was born on the twenty-eighth day of June, 1862, at Norristown. He was educated in the private schools of Harrisburg and Philadelphia. Entered the University of Pennsylvania in 1882, and is a member of the Fraternity of Delta Psi. From 1886 he was connected in business with his father until the death of the latter in 1889. He has always taken great interest in politics. Has been engaged in many campaigns of recent years, particularly that in Pennsylvania in 1890; the one in which William McKinley was elected Governor of Ohio in 1891; the Presidential campaign of 1892, and again in Ohio in 1893. His speeches have covered a wide territory: Pennsylvania, Ohio, New York and Connecticut, and have received marked attention and flattering notice. Mr. Hartranft is a member of the Union Republican and Young Republican Clubs of Philadelphia.

LINN HARTRANFT.

Culled from his speeches in the great campaign are the following extracts :

In the Peninsula Campaign the gallant old Spaniard who defended with determined valor, with a garrison of 6000 men, the Citadel of Ciudad Rodrigo, against Marshal Massena's army of 70,000 veteran French troops, managed after six weeks' desperate defence, with a worn-out garrison and shattered walls, to get through the lines of the besiegers a note to the Duke of Wellington, which contained these words only : "O, come ! Now ! now ! to the succor of this place." And two days later, in the last extremity, another, which repeated, "Now ! now ! For the last time."

From thousands of workshops, whose hearths are cold and machinery rusting ; from hundreds of thousands of homes, once the abode of plenty and contentment, whose bread-winners are now idle, and whose women and children sit with gaunt and anxious faces, comes to you, to all of us, my fellow-citizens, the cry, "Now ! to our help." Let our answer be given in next November.

The present political situation reminds me of the weather. We never have weather that pleases everybody, but we very frequently have weather that pleases nobody. The McKinley Bill could not please everybody, but it is certain that the present Democratic measure pleases nobody.

It was the third maxim of the great Napoleon, the world-acknowledged master in the art of war, "Never do what your enemy wants you to do, and simply because he wants you to do it." England has been our industrial rival since the settlement of this country, and has for years been looking with envious eyes at our home markets, of which our system of protection has been the only defence. She knows, if we do not, that if we give up our home markets, we will be doing exactly what our industrial rivals want us to do, and get absolutely nothing in return.

ONE afternoon four years ago, during the Gubernatorial campaign, a clergyman entered a railroad car at Harrisburg holding a newspaper clipping in his hand. He asked for Thomas J. Stewart, then candidate for Secretary of Internal Affairs. Approaching the colonel he said :

"I want to thank you, sir, for what you said in your address at Gettysburg yesterday. It is the most eloquent utterance I have ever read. I have clipped the speech out of the newspaper where I read it this morning and I am taking it home to my boy. He shall commit it to memory word by word. I wish every American boy in the land could do the same. I thank you again for your eloquent and patriotic utterance."

That was the way one of Colonel Thomas J. Stewart's utterances touched the heart of one man. He has touched thousands in just that same way. There are times when his eloquence lifts itself almost to the sublime, and then with that swift

GENERAL THOMAS J. STEWART,
Adjutant General.

transition that is so marked in the emotions of those of the Irish race, he turns the tears of sympathy into dewdrops of laughter. For years past no Grand Army gathering of any consequence, State or national, has been felt complete without the presence of "Tom" Stewart, as he is familiarly called by the old boys. His command of a rich, genteel brogue in the telling of an Irish yarn, or the inimicable mimicry of his German dialect is something beyond description; it is the foil to his superb eloquence and descriptive powers.

He was a lad just out of knickerbockers when he went to the war. He was born near Belfast, Ireland, September 11, 1848, and was brought by his parents to Norristown the following year. He received his education in the public schools, and after his discharge from the army he attended the Quaker City Business College. Then he drifted into the glass business in which he was engaged up to the time he entered public life as a State official. He has been Assistant Adjutant General, Department of Pennsylvania, G. A. R., member of the National Guard of Pennsylvania since 1869; elected to the Legislature in 1884; and elected Secretary of Internal Affairs in 1890–92, and now becomes Adjutant General of the State troops under Governor Hastings.

There have been shadows and scars on the life of Thomas J. Stewart, put there by struggles that time will never fully efface; but he has faced them with a brave heart and no one can say of him that there is a shadow or scar on his character as a man.

It is only necessary here to reproduce a few fragments of his many eloquent utterances. They serve as a shining beacon to show people who have never heard him what they have missed :

> The question of to-day is not one of politics, but of patriotism; not of blind devotion to party, but of love of home, and contentment and progress; not of cheap things and of cheap men, but of work, at fair wages, of dignified labor and manly men. And no party has ever been so fully and so truly the friend of labor, and of the workingman, and of all people, poor and rich alike, as the Republican party. It was born to release the shackled hand of the toiler, and its accomplished policies have made him a man, and given him power to do all things that become honest freemen. Its object, its very creation, was for the establishment and maintenance of human freedom. All men who believe in human liberty, who believe in the American nation and the American home, who believe in the elevation and dignity of labor, who believe in placing the possibility of home, and comfort and education within reach of all men, are at heart Republican.

On one occasion a very eloquent Irish divine announced that he would deliver a series of sermons on the miracles. In the front pew on a certain Sunday evening sat a very interested listener to the sermon on the miracle of the loaves and fishes. The clergyman became very earnest and said:

"F'what great miracles hev bin performed. Think uf it! No man iver done it before, and no one will iver do it agin. Pay attention to the impossibility." Then in an impressive way, he said : "An' He fed five people wid five tousand loaves."

Pat, sitting in the front pew, shrugged his shoulders, and said in an undertone: "Och! that's noathin'; I cud do that mesilf."

The clergyman heard the remark, and was puzzled as to his meaning, not knowing he had transposed the facts. Thinking it over during the week, he resolved to preach on the following Sunday a second sermon on the loaves and fishes. Pat was in his accustomed place. The clergyman began the sermon, in the meanwhile watching Pat closely. He repeated the statement of the former Sunday.

"What wonderful things wer' done! Think of it! No man iver dun it before, and no man will iver do it agin— He fed five tousand people wid five loaves." Then, pointing his finger at Pat, said: "Now, Murphy, cud you do that?"

"I cud," said Pat,

"You cud?"

"I cud."

"How, in the name of sinse, how?" said the clergyman.

"Why, your riverince," said Pat, "I would use what I had over from lasht Sunday."

The Republican party left enough wealth and prosperity and advancement and statesmanship in this land in 1892 to have carried the Democratic party through until 1896. There was enough left over had they been content to let well enough alone; but their policy was that of the destroyer, their statesmanship the kind that obstructs, and leads to national dishonor and humiliation.

We have been in distress, have been wandering in the valley of Democratic despair, the future seemed dark, but there is a bright light ahead. The Republican hosts are marching to victory. The sunshine is breaking through the clouds Under Republican rule, under Republican Protection, and by wise Republican statesmanship, this nation will again gather national blessings like unto a great harvest, and progress, and advancement and honor will again be her portion. Her homes will be happy, her hearthstones bright, her spindles humming, her furnaces blazing, and her anvils ringing. Her fields of waving grain, like a great ocean of gold, will yield rich return to the thrifty husbandman. The night of Democratic disaster will have been passed, and we shall be smiling and happy in the dawning of the better day that is so surely coming. Contentment, sunshine, prosperity, honor, everywhere and all the time. The blessings of protection to American industry, protection to American home and American labor and American capital, will fall on the land as softly and sweetly as tho' they came from the wings of an unseen dove. Let us press on to the victory that so surely awaits! Resolve that we shall do our part in the contest! Forward along the whole line! Every arm new nerved, every hand willing, every heart filled with hope and enthusiasm, every eye on the flag that tells the story of Republican loyalty and devotion. On thro' the Free Trade army, over the hosts of incompetency, to the new Appomattox that will mark a victory whose trophies will not be torn standards or stacked arms, but revived and rejuvenated industries, whose blazing furnaces shall light the way, and whose rolling wheels and roaring machinery shall tell of the return of American labor to its rightful home from the beggarly wanderings of the armies of want and anger!

IT was up in the beautiful little city of Bloomsburg that a new element in Pennsylvania politics came upon the scene. When the party
arrived at the hotel they found a large crowd in
waiting. Circulating through the assemblage of
stalwart Republicans and
reformed Democrats from
the "Fishing Creek Con-
federacy," was a young
man whom everybody fa-
miliarly addressed as
"Farmer." He looked
anything but a farmer.
His name was subsequent-
ly learned to be Monroe
H. Kulp, and the nick-
name "Farmer" an affec-
tionate sort of appellation
which the people of three
counties had given him
in years gone by. It is
perhaps a fact that one-
half of the people who
speak of Mr. Kulp as
"Farmer" Kulp really
believe that he is a farmer
or else that the title is his given name.

HON. MONROE H. KULP.

While Mr. Kulp was busy making the acquaintance of new friends and greeting old ones,

96

as the Republican candidate of the Seventeenth District, the depot 'bus drove up to the door. A fragile looking old man, with thin tragedian-like features, wiry build and dark eyes, stepped briskly down from the vehicle and hurried through the surging crowds into the hotel. He wore sober black garments, a queer little Billycock hat, and carried a worn gripsack in his hand. It was Republican day in Bloomsburg, and there was not a soul to welcome Charles R. Buckalew, Mr. Kulp's venerable Democratic opponent, in the throng. It was to Charles R. Buckalew a foretaste of defeat ; the first defeat that was to come to a Democrat in that famous Seventeenth hidebound Democratic District. It was the first and last meeting of the rivals during the campaign. It was under such circumstances that "Farmer" Kulp first presented himself to the gaze of the spellbinders.

The man who could win a desperate fight in the Seventeenth Congressional District and who will be a conspicuous figure in Congress is worth more than a casual notice. Monroe H. Kulp is only thirty-eight years of age. He is the eldest son of the late Darlington R. Kulp. He was born in Berks County, but since he was seven years of age has lived in Shamokin. He received a common school education between times when he was employed around his father's mines, working in every branch of the coal industry. Then he became interested in the lumber industry and made a study of that. His education was not what he desired, and so in 1879 he entered the State Normal College, at Lebanon, O., and in 1881 completed his collegiate life at Eastman College, Poughkeepsie, N. Y.

Mr. Kulp was practically at the head of his father's great business interests for some years previous to the latter's death. Since that time he has had all departments of the estates' allied interests at his finger ends. He employs over four hundred men, and does an annual business exceeding a quarter of a million dollars.

"Farmer" Kulp has always been popular. That was why he was nominated on first ballot by the congress of Northumberland County and why he was made the unanimous choice of the congress of the whole district.

So effectually did Mr. Kulp conduct his campaign that when the ballots were counted it was shown that he had caused a change of over 6200 votes from the vote of two years before. He was elected by a plurality of nearly 900, leading the splendid record of the State ticket by over 1500 votes.

AT the midnight mass-meeting at Coalport the last speaker was perhaps the youngest in the crowd that stood on the car platform. He came last because it was in his county, practically under his direction that the meeting was held. W. Irvin Shaw was his name and he was the chairman of the Clearfield Republican County Committee. Mr. Shaw is slight in figure, but active, sinewy, far-seeing and keenly alive to every move on the political chessboard in his district. It was this, with his attention to detail, that rolled up such an unprecedented Republican tide in November in that Democratic stronghold.

Mr. Shaw is a native of Clearfield and he was never prouder of his birthplace than after the polls closed on the sixth of last November. As a result of his splendid war, he has been again placed in charge of the Republican organization of the county. He is a college-bred man, coming from the public schools, entering Lafayette and later attending Yale Law School. He was admitted to the Clearfield bar in 1883, then went to Minneapolis, practiced in the State and district courts of Minnesota. After a few years he returned to Houtzdale, where he has practiced his profession with admirable success. Mr. Shaw is only thirty-four years of age, but in these

W. IRVIN SH.

short years he has crowded the political experience of double the count. He is a member of the Houtzdale school board and is president of the School Directors' Association of his county.

It is to be regretted that none of Mr. Shaw's campaign utterances can be reproduced. He speaks without notes, and as no detailed report of the speeches at the Coalport meeting was taken, his address, with the other notable ones, has gone into oblivion with the unrecorded good things of the great campaign.

"ADAM."

WHO of the tourists will ever forget "Adam?" Adam, the faithful bearer of bundles and custodian of "grips." Adam, who was the envy of every colored man in every town where a caravanserie covered the heads of the party. Adam Quander, Pittsburg, Pa., was his full name and address. He was the General's valet, and at odd intervals the caretaker of overcoats. Honest, faithful, cheerful, Adam never got left. May he never get left in the journey of life!

The Midnight Mass Meeting.

The Midnight Mass Meeting.

THE most remarkable feature of this remarkable campaign was the midnight mass meeting at Coalport. It was unique in the history of politics, State and national. Yet not a line about it ever got into print because of the lateness of the hour at which it was held, and the failure of the telegraph company promptly to deliver the only story of the event which was written and sent over the wires from the scene of the gathering.

The meeting was held at 12.30 o'clock on the morning of October 10, at the town of Coalport, on the Bell's Gap Railroad. From 400 to 500 people, men and women, were present. Ten speeches were made in less than an hour. There is a romantic story behind it all that goes back a dozen years.

—-

Years ago, no matter how long, a young man came to General Hastings at his home in Bellefonte and told him how he had been discharged from his place as station agent for some slight infraction of rules. The future looked dark, for he had a young wife on his hands, and he was in debt. With all his sympathies aroused by the story, General Hastings promised to do all he could toward securing him another situation. Letters were written to various railroad friends and within a short time, through the influence of Mr. Hastings, the young man was given employment at Coalport.

The years went by, and the incident had been forgotten by Daniel H. Hastings. When Punxsutawney was reached the General received a hurriedly written letter. It was a request from the man he had helped years before. It called to mind the friendly aid that had been extended by the candidate years before; that now an opportunity was presented to, in a measure, repay that debt, and if General Hastings and his party would only stop their special train at Coalport on their way to ex-Governor Curtin's funeral, they would be greeted by the greatest mass meeting of its citizens in the history of the town. No matter if it was midnight, if Hastings would stop, the people would be there.

Such an appeal was irresistible. The special did stop. Every member of the party made an address, and General Hastings took personal charge of the meeting. The story as told in the special dispatch to the Philadelpha *Press*, written by a smoky lamp in the depot at Coalport while the meeting was in progress, and which never reached its destination, is given in full below :

COALPORT, 10, 10, '94.
To the Philadelphia Press:

In the varied history of Pennsylvania politics nothing approaching to-night's incident was ever experienced. It is now 12.30 o'clock in the morning and a full-fledged and specially arranged mass meeting is in progress here. General Hastings and the speakers of his party are addressing 500 enthusiastic men and women by the blaze of torch-lights. It came about in this way:

Coalport is in Clearfield County, on the railroad to Bellwood, forty-nine miles from Punxsutawney. When it became known, this afternoon, that General Hastings would pass through the town after midnight on a special train, the telegraph wires were set to work and an invitation extended him to stop off. He consented by wire. Immediately large posters were run off in a Coalport printing office, and at six o'clock every citizen of the place was notified of the early morning meeting.

The special, in charge of W. M. Erwine, trainmaster, left Punxsutawney at eleven o'clock. When the train drew into the station at Coalport a great bonfire was blazing, its flames shooting twenty feet into the air. A brass band was playing, men were beating on boiler iron, and dynamite cartridges were exploded with startling effect. To the astonishment of the party on the special they discovered that at least one quarter of the audience were ladies, who waved handkerchiefs and cheered with enthusiasm.

As I write the meeting is in full blast, with the entire force of speakers in General Hastings' party addressing the enthusiastic assemblage from the rear platform of Superintendent Ford's private car. General Hastings is in charge of the meeting. He speaks of the event as being unparalleled in the history of Pennsylvania politics. He is introducing in succession, General Latta, Major George Orlady, W. I. Schaffer, Wilbur F. Reeder, General Hastings' law partner, Hon. Jerome B. Niles, Congressman Brosius, Hon. Lyman D. Gilbert, Congressman Hicks, W. C. Arnold, Congressional candidate in this district, and W. I. Shaw, County Chairman of Clearfield, all of whom make five-minute speeches.

The people are intensely enthusiastic and greet each speaker with cheers. The meeting, under arrangement with Trainmaster Erwine, is to last fifty minutes. The time is up within ten minutes, and not a single auditor has left. Each speaker refers briefly to the tariff issue and in highly complimentary terms to the fidelity to Republicanism and the sincere enthusiasm of the people of Coalport. The announcement of Mr. Orlady that General Hastings will be elected by 200,000, as a rebuke to the free-trade Democracy, is greeted with repeated cheers.

General Hastings is holding a reception, while the band plays "Red, White and Blue," the crowd joining in the chorus.

(Signed.)   G. N. McC.

Next to the famous midnight mass meeting at Coalport, the oddest meeting was that held at Claysville, a suburb of Punxsutawney. It was a grotesque mingling of past and present. Two o'clock in the afternoon was the hour set. A trolley car, decked with dazzling gorgeousness in red, white and blue bunting, drew up to the hotel. In front of the car was a martial band. Preceding the band were fifty citizens wearing badges, and in advance of the whole line was a young man astride of a splendid black horse, with a great flag over his shoulder, trailing down to the ground. Behind the car were one hundred more men wearing badges.

But what a contrast of eras between that trolley car and drum corps. One fifer—there were two of them—was a weather-beaten veteran of the great rebellion, who wore his Grand Army hat in honor of the occasion. Of the three drummers one was a graybeard with halting step, who, thirty years before, had beaten the reveille, in the battle years, in the fertile valleys of Virginia. On one side of him marched a young man of twenty, while on the other staggered along, beneath the weight of a great old-fashioned snare-drum, a little lad not yet in his teens. General Hastings rode on the front platform, beside the motorman.

Business was temporarily suspended at Claysville during the meeting. The schools took a recess and the stores closed. Two store boxes were pushed out on the edge of the sidewalk, and mounted upon these, the speakers, General Hastings, Hon. Jerome B. Niles, Major Orlady and Congressman Brosius, addressed the assemblage, which thronged the dusty street. The shoemaker stood near, wearing his leather apron; the storekeeper was in his shirt sleeves; the farmers, whip in hand, left their wagons in the street and pushed up close on the outskirts of the crowd. Then the old and the new, the trolley car and the war-time drummers, with the grizzled old veteran beating out "Yankee Doodle" on the bass drum with two sticks, and the baby drummer staggering along with his snare-drum, led the way back, through the rows of flags and lanterns on the houses, to the hotel.

General Hastings got into the greatest crush of the campaign at Punxsutawney. Fully two thousand people had gathered outside the opera house. The mob surrounded him and his escorts in hilarious welcome. He could get neither backward nor forward. His hat was jammed over his eyes, his friends became separated, and he was helpless in the midst of a good-natured, cheering crowd. Then the doors opened and the candidate was borne along, seemingly on the crest of a human tide, and literally hurled into the auditorium of the building.

Punxsutawney was the most gorgeously decorated town encountered on the trip. Enthusiastic residents on Mahoning street had the flower beds on their lawns marked out with tiny flags. At night rows of incandescent lights blazed along cornice and porch roof. Even the dogs had bows of red, white and blue tied on their tails,

It was the only campaign ever known in the State of Pennsylvania in which the warfare was carried across the Delaware into New Jersey.

On the day that General Hastings was announced to speak at Easton, a great parade of firemen took place at Philipsburg, just across the river, in New Jersey. A score of Pennsylvania companies of red-shirted fire-fighters participated in the rally. Half the population of Easton trooped across the old covered bridge to swell the throng. General Hastings and his party went with the crowd. As his carriage drove up the long avenue of the New Jersey town, his familiar face was recognized and he was frequently cheered. When the carriage stopped near the reviewing stand, it was instantly surrounded, and for a few minutes he held an impromptu reception.

"Ef I can't vote fer him, I kin, b'gosh, shake hands with him an' wish him well," exclaimed one old Jerseyman, with a sober wag of his grizzly head.

Schuylkill County gave the General the busiest day of the campaign. A special train swept the party around sharp curves, past culm banks, over mountains and beside swift flowing rivers, with stops every few miles for speech making, until, when night came, everybody was about ready to drop with fatigue.

On this day General Hastings was the central figure in one of the most touching episodes of the whole campaign. It occurred at Girardville, and there was not the slightest trace or hint of politics in the whole bright episode.

The public school in Girardville is located on the main street. It is surrounded by a low iron fence. As the Hastings party came up the street this fence was transformed into a living wall. Two hundred boys and girls with bright, eager faces lined its length, shouting and waving caps and handkerchiefs. It was not in the heart of any man, much less of the big-hearted Republican standard-bearer, to decline such an ovation. The carriage was halted and General Hastings dismounted. The men with the banners and the committeemen and visitors stood outside on the curb. Politics halted this side the school yard fence. General Hastings stepped inside the gate to a burst of juvenile applause that was heard a square away up to the Reading tracks. As he stood bareheaded, and towering above them all he was surrounded by a pushing, shouting throng. The Principal introduced General Hastings to the children, and instantly the hand clapping and applause was redoubled. When it had subsided the General said :

Boys and girls, I want to say that for the past three weeks I have been hearing night and day the music of brass bands and the applause of men, but in all that time I have heard nothing that was so sweet and so pleasant to my ears as your applause this afternoon. Nothing so beautiful has appeared to me as this array of happy faces by which I am surrounded. I hope that you will all be blessed with long and useful lives; that you will get all the sunshine out of your lives that you can and that you will always be proud of, and faithful to, the flag of your country which is flying over your heads to-day. Goodbye.

There was another impulsive burst of applause and shrill cheers, and then it seemed as if General Hastings was the centre of a whirlpool of children. The boys and girls finally got into the semblance of a line, and for ten minutes the General was kept busy shaking hands and saying pleasant things to his little friends. And meantime the men with the banners and the men with the badges and the brass band and the politicians remained outside the school yard fence on the curbstone.

Reading will be remembered as the place where General Hastings was first named as a Presidential possibility. Cyrus G. Derr was the man, the Opera House the place, and the date September 29.

Towanda, the "Pools," the brass band, and any one of the greatest out-door audiences of any campaign are linked together. As to the "Pools," a corruption of Vanderpool, they are a remarkable community in Bradford County. They are not an ornament to that congressional district. They are nondescript children of mixed blood; of New-Amsterdam Dutch and Pennsylvania Indian and Virginia Negro, and the

THE "POOLS" ON DRESS PARADE.

Lord only knows what else, so they say up there. Their origin dates from the beginning of this century; perhaps farther back. At all events the Pools, by whatever other name they are known, are with few exceptions, about on a par with the "Crackers" of Georgia, and the Clay Eaters of the Carolinas. Fair time in Towanda sees the Pools in all their glory. They come to town in droves, and on this day they were there by scores, the cynosure of the strangers' eyes.

The brass band on that afternoon at Towanda was a dream. Its music was all right, but its make-up in point of uniform, discounted any comic opera band ever seen. There were four uniforms to twelve men, each man got something, if only a vest or cap, until it came down to the bass drummer. He had to be content with a pair of epaulets and a white belt.

Beaver Falls was the place where rival hotels clamored for the honor of entertaining the candidates. To preserve good feeling all around, dinner

was taken at one hotel and supper at another.
As there was no third claimant for the privilege
of bedding the party, the managers deemed it
advisable, to avoid hard feeling, to ship the outfit
to Pittsburg on a midnight train.

Hastings threw dignity to the wind for two
minutes in Greenville. The Opera House was
packed and breathless. The General had out-
lined the good words and works of the Republican
party during its thirty years of triumph. Then
after depicting the Democratic triumph at the
polls two years ago, and raising one hand dramati-
cally above his head, he exclaimed with impressive
earnestness:

"And since then what has the Democratic
party been doing?"

From a distant corner of the gallery the answer
came with prompt and startling distinctness:

"Raising hell, principally."

Hanging over the balcony front at the great
Wilkesbarre meeting were some scores of hilarious young men. They had lungs of leather, and
the enthusiasm of four counties. To every out-
burst of applause they tacked on this refrain, with
all the precision of a college cry:

"Who are we? who are we?
Gallery Gods for Hastings! See!"

Johnsonburg felt that the exigencies of the occasion demanded the patriotic exhibition of all her varied resources. Hence the base-ball club, in full uniform, turned out to welcome the campaigning party.

Bloomsburg filled her Court House and Opera House to their capacity. Three excursion trains and three brass bands added to the clamor. It was the greatest exhibition of pure, unadulterated enthusiasm seen during any campaign, because there was not an ounce of red fire or a single Roman candle or rocket let off during that memorable night.

HON. JAMES S. McKEAN.

The Charleroi meeting in point of enthusiasm, crowd and earnestness of purpose, was the climax of the great campaign. Its success was largely due to Hon. James S. McKean, ex-postmaster of Pittsburg. With indefatigable zeal he labored to make it the political event in the history of Western Pennsylvania politics. And he succeeded.

Charleroi is the city of a day. The realization of an Arabian night's dream. Five years ago its streets were wheat fields. The magic wand of capital touched it and fences fell and factories rose. To-day it has one of the greatest glass factories in the world within its limits. Its population is numbered by thousands. By whatever name it may be called, the Magic city, or the Dream city, it is one of the wonders of our American civilization. It is intensely Republican because it is a manufacturing city. When it prepared to welcome General Hastings it sent invitations to the people of other States. They came in hundreds by excursion trains, in squads, by wagons, and in cavalcades on horseback. Steamboats towing barges filled with shouting coal miners came from down stream and up the river. Maryland sent delegations; West Virginia was represented, and thirty car loads of Pittsburg enthusiasts swelled the throng.

The daylight parade required twenty-five minutes to pass a given point. The town was swathed in bunting. All doors were opened to visitors ; even the churches spread hospitable tables. The meeting was held on a vast plateau overlooking the valley of the Monongahela. Under the spreading branches of great trees a wide platform accommodating 500 distinguished people was erected.

10,000 people massed in front of it. John P. Eberhart, a representative workingman, presided, and the speakers were General Hastings, Major George B. Orlady and Hon. Charles F. Warwick. The transparencies were unique. On the platform were gathered all of the candidates on the State ticket except Congressman Grow and Hon. Amos Mylin. The Charleroi meeting was the greatest political gathering ever held, outside of Pittsburg, west of the Allegheny Mountains.

The Norristown discussion was the unique finale of this unique campaign. General D. H. Hastings addressed the Democratic mass meeting in the court house, and was followed by Colonel William M. Singerly. Then the party was driven to the Opera House, where Colonel Singerly addressed the assembled Republicans, and in turn was followed by General Hastings.

It all came about in this way: Colonel Singerly and General Hastings have been friends for years. Throughout the campaign not a single word had been uttered by either gentleman that would grate harshly upon the feelings of the other. It was a campaign conducted upon a high moral plane; remarkable in that respect from any other campaign, perhaps, in the history of Pennsylvania. When an invitation came, therefore, from Colonel Singerly to General Hastings to a joint discussion at Norristown, the invitation was promptly accepted and arrangements perfected.

Colonel Alexander K. McClure, the distinguished editor of the Philadelphia *Times*, and a warm personal friend of each candidate, extended an invitation to Colonel Singerly and General Hastings and to their friends to accompany him in his special car from Philadelphia to Norristown, on the evening of the joint debate, November 3. The exigencies of the campaign compelled both of the distinguished candidates to precede Colonel McClure's party to Norristown. Those who accepted the hospitality of Colonel and Mrs. McClure were Mrs. Daniel H. Hastings, Colonel B. F. Gilkeson, Chairman of the Republican State Committee, and Mrs. Gilkeson, Hon. Charles Emory Smith and Mrs. Smith, Secretary of the Commonwealth William F. Harrity and Mrs. Harrity, Colonel and Mrs. James H. Lambert, Hon. George S. Graham and Mrs. Graham, Dr. and Mrs. George V. Shoemaker, Hon. Walter Lyon, Republican candidate for Lieutenant Governor, Mrs. Singerly Balch, Miss Singerly Meredith, Hon. William Littleton and Miss Littleton, Congressman George F. Huff, Mr. and Mrs. Lewis E. Beitler, Mr. and Mrs. George N. McCain, General James W. Latta, Republican candidate for Secretary of Internal Affairs, the Misses Frasel, Mrs. W. I. Schaffer, Miss Chisholm and Miss Cheston.

It is not the purpose to give here in detail any of the features of the discussion. The vast audiences were delighted. Each candidate was treated with that courtesy and distinguished consideration to which he was entitled. When the two candidates faced thousands of rival partisans and clasped hands amid tumultuous cheers, the waving of thousands of flags, and in the presence of hundreds of fair women, they did so without the sacrifice of a single political principle. The other speakers of the evening, indoor and out, were Hon. Charles Emory Smith, General James W. Latta, Major Orlady, and Hon. George S. Graham.

Upon the return of the candidates and their friends to the city they were entertained at a very charming luncheon given by Mrs. General D. H. Hastings at the Hotel Stratford. Thus the memorable campaign of 1894, so far as the State was concerned, was closed.

Guests of the Tour.

GUESTS OF THE TOUR.

THE pleasure, whatever there was of it, in the excitement of vast cheering crowds, waving flags and banners, and brass band melodies, Daniel H. Hastings was not content to retain solely to himself. One of the distinguishing characteristics of the standard-bearer of the Republican party in the great campaign, was his constant solicitude for the welfare of others. No man who traveled in any capacity with him for twenty-four hours will gainsay this assertion. In it lies one secret of the great personal affection which men in their individual capacity, separate and apart from politics, have for "big Dan of the Middle Mountain." There were rough places in the way sometimes, when nerves were jarred, and teeth set on edge, and sensibilities shocked, but General Hastings, with that keen instinctive delicacy of feeling for others, always smoothed out the wrinkles of circumstance and speech, as best he could, and by every means in his power strove to make the crooked paths straight.

So it came about that when the campaign reached a climacteric stage, when the State was blazing with enthusiasm, he sent for personal friends; men who had stood by him, and whom he had known in years past, to join the party and share in its pleasurable triumphs. Among these was General J. K. Robison, of Juniata County, the first Hastings delegate in the State, a charming old gentleman, with a splendid war record. Colonel J. P. Coburn, of Centre County, a Republican without fear and without reproach, who bore the scars of party conflict and had passed under the fire of enthusiasm in great national conventions, was another.

DURING the last two weeks of the campaign, while General Hastings was busy in Philadelphia, a tall young gentleman in a tall silk hat, a short, dark moustache and a very wide acquaintance came upon the scene. He took almost a paternal interest in the General. He arranged for special trains, pacified impatient interviewers, received visitors and acted generally as Governor Hastings' *alter ego*.

Everybody in the world of politics knows him as Lewis Eugene Beitler, the most accomplished private secretary in public life in Pennsylvania to-day, and a gentleman whose tact is only equaled by his unfailing courtesy.

It is possible that no single man in public life to-day is the possessor of so many secrets, political and private, as Mr. Beitler. He has served through two terms as private secretary and confidential friend to two mayors of Philadelphia, Edwin H. Fitler and Edwin S. Stuart. And with no other man are those secrets so safe. One of the wisest acts of his pre-administration days on Governor Hastings' part was the selection of Mr. Beitler as his private secretary.

LEWIS EUGENE BEITLER.

Mr. Beitler is just past thirty-one. He is a brother of Director of Public Safety Abraham M. Beitler. He is a graduate of the public schools, and was the orator at the Grammar Schools commencement. He is also a graduate of the Franklin Institute, Department of Drawing and was a law student at the University of Pennsylvania.

Under the most trying circumstances in the past Mr. Beitler has developed his ability to manage men so that harsh blows fall with softened force. He is unalterably loyal to his friends, a wise, cool counselor, and under all circumstances a gentleman. He is happily married.

ONE day about the third week in the campaign, a medium-sized, slenderly-built gentleman, with dark moustache and keen eyes, joined the combination. He was exceedingly modest, and for a day or two did not meet all of the combination. As he became better known, the sterling worth of the man became appreciated. He was secretary of the Republican County Committee of Centre County, a close and valuable friend of General Hastings, as his frequent conferences and the confidence which the General reposed in him testified. Such was Wilmer L. Malin, of Bellefonte, superintendent of the Central Pennsylvania Telephone and Supply Company, of Williamsport. Mr. Malin, who is a Chester Countian by birth, is forty-four years of age, and from 1868 to 1883 was manager of Pennsylvania Railroad and Western Union Telegraph offices. For a dozen years he has been actively interested in

Centre County politics. During General Hastings' preliminary contest for the nomination, four years ago, Mr. Malin visited ten counties in the State in his behalf. He has been the intimate political friend of General Hastings for a dozen years. As a political worker, his value is shown in the fact that in the ten counties visited by him in behalf of General Hastings all of them gave the General their delegates or the delegation was divided with him. Because of his excellent judgment, his energy, his warm personal friendship, and his absolute integrity, he has been one of General Hastings' most discreet and valuable friends.

WILMER L. MALIN.

ANOTHER valuable friend, whose advice was frequently invoked was Major Levi G. McCauley, the Republican leader of Chester County. Long years of intimate association with Major McCauley had proven his value not only to General Hastings, but to many members of his party. The Major is a man with a history; a history of warfare in which political battles are as the assaults of tin soldiers. His empty right sleeve is the testimonial to his patriotism, his valor and his splendid spirit of self-sacrifice. Here, in brief, is the war story in the life of a man who is known in every county in the State, and whose services to the party have been pre-eminent in their value:

Mustered into the service June 13, 1861, as a

MAJOR LEVI G. McCAULEY.

private in Company F, Seventh Pennsylvania Reserves. Was made a sergeant in a few days, then first lieutenant. He was with his regiment in all the battles before Richmond. At Charles City Cross Roads he lost his right arm, was taken prisoner and sent to Libby. He was mustered out June 30, 1866, and brevetted major for gallantry on the field. As county chairman of Chester County he gave General Harrison the greatest vote ever given a candidate in that county, viz., 11,578. He was one of the original Hastings men.

"I WANT you to come along with us for a few days. There is no reason why you cannot. I want you to see how the Republicans of Pennsylvania are aroused in this campaign. Come, now, I will not take no for an answer!"

Such an invitation was irresistible, coming as it did from the head of the Republican State ticket. The man to whom it was addressed is one of the most prominent Republicans in Eastern Pennsylvania, Hon. J. C. Brown, editor of the *Columbia County Republican*. Unassuming and modest in his manner, yet possessing an energy of expression that finds vent in the eloquence and wit of political address, Mr. Brown was one of the most genial guests in the entire tour. His life history has been varied. He has been a public school teacher, college professor, civil engineer and editor. He is a

HON. J. C. BROWN.

graduate and degree man of Dickinson Seminary, and was the valedictorian of his class. Was professor in the Bloomsburg Literary Institute and part of the time principal. Surveyed the line of the North and West Branch Railroad, and as assistant or chief has been employed in engineering work for nearly every railroad in Northeastern Pennsylvania in recent years. His first active interest in politics was manifested in the Hartranft campaign of 1872. Since then he has filled nearly every political office from State delegate and county chairman to national delegate. The high esteem in which he is held by his townsmen is shown in the fact that he has been a member of the Bloomsburg School Board since 1878. He is also one of the trustees of the State Normal School at that place. As a campaign orator he has a State reputation.

TEN days before the campaign closed, a plainly dressed man, wearing a soft brown hat and a sandy goatee, walked down the aisle of the spellbinders' car, as it stood in the Reading Terminal Station, at Philadelphia, paused near its centre, and looking around upon the assembled spellbinders and statesmen, deeply immersed in their newspapers, exclaimed in a clear, penetrating voice of peculiar intonation, with a broad smile on his face:

"Oh! why should the spirit of mortal be proud?"

"Hello, Cooper," came from all quarters of the car, in all sorts of voices, and in a moment Thomas Valentine Cooper, ex-President of the State Senate, and the man with the longest record of continuous service in that distinguished body, was shaking hands, with both hands, with the friends and admirers who gathered about him.

HON. THOMAS V. COOPER.

In one way ex-Senator Cooper was the most striking figure, other than the candidates, during the closing days of the campaign. He made no speeches outside his own county, except one or two, perhaps, and he accompanied the party as a distinguished guest, at the invitation of General Hastings. He was a striking figure, though, because he had helped to make history that will be memorable in parliamentary circles for all time to come. Legislative hand-books, for nearly a score of years, have been publishing biographical sketches of Senator Cooper to an extent that excuses their repetition here. One incident, striking in its effect, and indicative of the shrewd, far-seeing policy of this leader of his party in the Senate, is worth repeating.

Thomas V. Cooper has few peers as a parliamentarian. In the extra session of '83 an incident occurred which anticipated by several years the celebrated decision of Tom Reed as to counting a quorum.

The Senate was dead-locked one day, there being but twenty-six Republicans present, and one of the number (Agnew, of Beaver) refused to vote for Cooper's resolution to rescind a previous resolution to the effect that the Legislature would not accept pay if the apportionment bills were not passed. This practically amounted to a loss of $1500 to each member if the legislation which Governor Pattison sought to compel was not passed.

Senator Cooper desired to rescind so as to leave all free to vote for the Republican bills, and to stick to them if vetoed. Senator Agnew sat silent, and as the Democrats also refused to vote, it left but twenty-five ayes—not a constitutional quorum, twenty-six being required. The usual calls exhausted the time until the noon recess, when Senator Reyburn said to Cooper that he believed those who called the yeas and nays were officially present whether they voted or not.

Senator Cooper said he had always believed the same, but there was nothing in the books to support the view. "However," he suggested, "if you will so decide, Reyburn, we will put you in the chair, and fight it out."

This was done in the afternoon. Senators Gordon and Kennedy called the yeas and nays, and Cooper raised the point of order, when later they refused to vote, that having called the yeas and nays they were present; Reyburn decided the point well taken. Then followed wild scenes on the Democratic side, but Senator Reyburn was firm, and Gordon and Kennedy were counted as present and voting.

Later in the day, Cooper, with a view to show how absurd was the Democratic opposition to this ruling, privately asked President Mylin to call Kennedy to the chair. When this was done, Cooper got up a sham fight, which looked real; Gordon and Humes called the yeas and nays, but refused to vote. Cooper made the same point of order, but Kennedy decided they were *not* present.

Cooper appealed, and when debating the appeal, suddenly and as though the thought had just occurred to him, withdrew the appeal and raised the point of order that the *Chair was present*, Kennedy's making the needed twenty-sixth vote. Kennedy had to decide that he himself was absent, not having voted.

Senator Wallace, a veteran parliamentarian, jumped up and said that the Democratic side of the contest had been so absurdly managed that he would no longer waste his time in attending the sessions.

Hon. Tom Reed's article in the *North American Review*, defending his decision, cited this Cooper case as conclusive in the matter. It reduced the doctrine of absence when not voting and present to an absurdity.

NO brighter example of the possibilities of our American life or of the self-reliance and courage of American youth can be shown than is displayed in the career of Lieutenant Wilbur F. Reeder, of the law firm of Hastings & Reeder, of Bellefonte. Occupying as he does to-day a distinguished place at the bar of Centre County, and a position of respect and esteem in the hearts of all who know him, Lieutenant Reeder can look back with pride on a career in life which

LIEUT. WILBUR F. REEDER.

stretches from the farm to the forum of legal distinction. He is a farmer's son, and like the majority of the professional men of this and every other State, gained his education in the common schools and completed it by becoming a public school teacher himself. He is still a young man, on the sunny side of forty-four, a Pennsylvanian by birth, and during his entire professional life, until within the past few years, has been associated with Daniel H. Hastings. The Governor-elect was his legal preceptor, and subsequently his partner. Lieutenant Reeder has been identified with the State militia for many years, and is now First Lieutenant of Company B, Fifth Regiment. The crown of his life and endeavors, however, is his home. Charming in its surroundings and perfect in its artistic adornment, it is graced by the presence of a wife and son whose devotion is all that heart can wish.

IT was when General Hastings' voice grew so weak and his throat so raw in the last week of the great campaign, that Dr. John Veitch Shoemaker and his little black satchel joined the spellbinders. But Dr. Shoemaker was a spellbreaker. He sprayed cooling lotions into the General's hot throat, felt his pulse, hammered his chest and took other medical liberties with him. But he enabled the General to finish his campaign.

We had heard of Dr. Shoemaker before. Schaffer, who seemed to possess an unsatisfiable craving for physic and drugs—seemed to thrive on the diet—always carried some loam-colored composition in gun-wad pellets, which he would flash forth, like a beadle with his snuff box, and invite all hands to have a dose with him, excusing himself by saying: " Dr. Shoemaker says I must take these for my stomach," or liver, or lights, as the case happened to be. Hence everybody knew the Doctor, embraced him and welcomed him to one night stands and three meetings a day.

The Doctor took kindly enough to it all. He didn't talk much the first day, but the second his timidity wore off. But one couldn't expect a distinguished physician to grow enthusiastic over crowds, and bands, and banners. And Dr. John Veitch Shoemaker is distinguished for so young a man. There is nothing in medical ethics to prevent an outsider saying this; nor in taking a chronological peep into his history.

Born Chambersburg, March 18, 1852. Graduated Dickinson College, 1868; M. A., 1875; M. D., Jefferson, 1874. Demonstrator of Anatomy same year at Jefferson;

1876, lecturer Philadelphia School of Anatomy; 1883, lecturer on diseases of the skin at Jefferson; 1886, professor skin diseases, Medico-Chirurgical; President American Medical Editors' Association; 1889, professor materia-medica and therapeutics, Medico-Chirurgical; three times delegate to International Medical Congresses in Europe; author numerous treatises on medical subjects, and editor of the *Times and Register.*

"Adam, where's the General?" inquired Major Orlady one day.

"Jes' gone to his room, Mist' Ohlady. Dr. Shoemaker's workin' th' itemizer on him, sa'."

He meant the atomizer.

Out at Phœnixville General Hastings spoke out of doors in a drizzling mist. Then he hurried into the hotel, where Dr. Shoemaker began spraying his throat. Down at the foot of the stairs stood a self-appointed guard, tall, lank, grizzled, abrupt and profane of speech, with cowhide boots and broom-handle cane.

"Can't gowup," and he glared at a visitor and thrust the broom-handle across the stairway to bar his ascent.

"I want to see the General."

"Can't gowup."

"Why?"

"Busy."

"What's he doing?"

"He haint doin' nothin', but there's a feller up there with a bellows an' piece of hose pumpin' wind 'r water down him, an' damfino which. Ye can't gowup."

And he didn't.

THE one man who has stood closest to General D. H. Hastings in the past half-dozen years in Eastern Pennsylvania, if not in the State, has been Colonel James H. Lambert, of the *Press*. He has been the staunch, unyielding friend of General Hastings under every circumstance and at all times. For this reason, if for no other, Colonel Lambert is entitled to place in these pages

COLONEL JAMES H. LAMBERT,
Insurance Commissioner.

as a more than guest, at various stages of the State tour, notably at Reading and at Norristown.

Colonel Lambert was born in Syracuse, N. Y., forty-nine years ago. He began life as a newsboy on the street, and between times picked up an education in the public schools. By natural association with the business he drifted after a while into a printing office as an apprentice. He worked at his trade in Michigan, whither his parents moved, then became a publisher of a newspaper himself. Through his newspaper connection he drifted into politics, and was elected to the Michigan Legislature before he was of age. He reached his majority ten days before the Legislature convened. After numerous vicissitudes as editor and publisher, he came to Pennsylvania as editor of the Williamsport *Gazette and Bulletin*. From there he came to the Philadelphia *Times* as an editorial writer, then as managing editor. He has been identified with the *Inquirer* as editor-in-chief, and is now, and has been for some years, the State political editor of the *Press*. He was a member of Governor Beaver's staff. Affable, yet dignified, inviting rather than giving confidences, he has more friends in political life than any other man in the State. To the gratification of these friends Colonel Lambert has been appointed Insurance Commissioner for the State in the cabinet of Governor Hastings.

The Historians.

THE HISTORIANS.

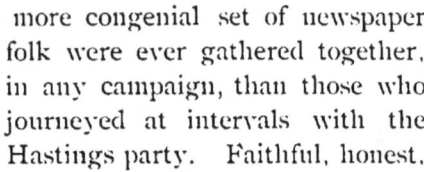

NO more congenial set of newspaper folk were ever gathered together, in any campaign, than those who journeyed at intervals with the Hastings party. Faithful, honest, conscientious gentlemen, every one of them. Men of broad and varied experience, with few exceptions, who love their profession, and who are gifted with that rare power of putting inspiration into the words which they pen.

Foremost among the number must be mentioned Mr. Howard H. Derr, of the Philadelphia *Record*. Representing, as he did, the newspaper owned and edited by Mr. William M. Singerly, the Democratic candidate for Governor, and a Democrat himself, Mr. Derr's position as a member of the Republican campaigning party was one of extreme delicacy. Yet from beginning to end he discharged his duty to his newspaper faithfully and honestly, and with a fairness to the Republican candidates and their friends which made for him some lasting friendships. What is true of Mr. Derr can also be said with equal candor of Mr. Peter Bolger, who, for a brief time, preceded Mr. Derr as the *Record's* historian with the Republican campaigning party. Among the other gentlemen of the newspaper profession were Hon. Henry Hall, representing the Pittsburg *Times*, concerning whose genial personality and oratorical gifts more appears elsewhere. Mr. John Gregg, also of the Pittsburg *Times*, was an acceptable addition to the party beyond the Alleghenies. Mr. A. R. Crum, the widely known legislative correspondent and political writer of the Pittsburg *Commercial Gazette*, spent several days as the guest of General Hastings.

HOWARD H. DERR.

Mr. James Israel, who for a number of years has been one of the bright particular stars of the Pittsburg *Dispatch*, journeyed across the State to describe the Norristown meeting in his clever descriptive way. Mr. Charles R. Dorworth, the Bellefonte correspondent of the Philadelphia *Inquirer*, represented that paper on the tour from start to finish. Mr. Stephen Bolles, of the Erie

Dispatch, was the party's historian for the Northwest, while in the Southeast, Mr. Louis N. Megargee, the Philadelphia *Times*' gifted special writer, and Mr. Peter Hoban, of the Philadelphia *Ledger*, told the story of the closing hours of the campaign in graphic lines.

To the hundreds of other newspaper men throughout the State, who participated in the great campaign in all its various stages, who must be nameless here, to them must be given the credit of immeasurable aid in bringing about the results of the great campaign, as witnessed at the closing of the polls on the sixth of November last.

GEORGE NOX MCCAIN.

The Social Side.

THE SOCIAL SIDE.

THE social features of the Hastings campaign were unique. Private hospitality opened wide its doors in nearly every town of importance where the campaign party halted for the night. A list of the personal friends and public-spirited citizens who entertained General Hastings and the members of his party, were they grouped together, would present a roster of distinguished names. Mr. W. J. McConnell, of Shamokin, one of the prominent citizens of that prosperous and progressive little city, gave a dinner that was one of the notable social features of the campaign. The menu was of the highest order, the service superb. The attractiveness of the table was enhanced by two great scroll-shaped banks of roses. The guests of the evening were General Hastings, General J. W. Latta, Major George B. Orlady, Hon. Charles F. Warwick, Hon.

W. J. McCONNELL, ESQ.

John B. Robinson, Monroe H. Kulp, C. O. Mc-
Williams, Linn Hartranft, Hon. Henry Hall, W.
I. Schaffer, Hon. Marriott Brosius and George N.
McCain.

Earlier on the same day the same party, with
the addition of Colonel J. P. Coburn, of Centre
County, Chairman H. A. Taylor, of Union
County, and Hon. B. F. Focht, were entertained
at luncheon by John F. Duncan, Esq., president
of the Republican League of Lewisburg, at his
beautiful home in that city. This occasion was
enhanced by the presence of a number of ladies
who had gathered in the parlors to welcome the
distinguished visitor.

There are memories that will always linger,
never to be forgotten, around the occasion of the
Curtin funeral. The home of Lieutenant Wilbur
F. Reeder furnishes one of these. It was here
that General Hastings and his friends were enter-
tained during their brief halt at the open grave of
the great war governor. The dinner table on
this occasion was graced by the presence of
General Hastings, Mr. Justice Dean, of the
Pennsylvania Supreme Court, Major Orlady,
Hon. Lyman D. Gilbert, Colonel Thomas J.
Stewart, Secretary of Internal Affairs, Gen-
eral J. W. Latta, Hon. Jerome B. Niles,
H. H. Derr and Geo. N. McCain.

Then there was the dinner which Mr. Simon Perkins, of Sharon, gave to General Hastings. Mr. Perkins is one of the great iron manufacturers of the Shenango Valley. He is not only interested in the economic theories of the Republican party, but he also strives to interest the intelligent men in his employ in them. The dinner served in his splendid home on the hillside overlooking the Sharon was unique. It was a welcome relief to the stereotyped bills of fare in country hotels. It was a home dinner with roast beef and mince pie, and buttermilk and cider. It was a dinner that in its substantial excellence will never be forgotten. To add to its interest was the fact that the heads of the departments in Mr. Perkins' great iron establishments were distributed around the table among the guests. It was one of the most enjoyable affairs of the whole campaign.

The story of the great Charleroi meeting would be incomplete without a testimonial to the gracious hospitality of its people. Mr. C. F. Thompson, brother-in-law of Hon. James S. McKean, ex-postmaster of Pittsburg, acted as host to General Hastings and his party on that day, although Mr. McKean shared the pleasant duties of host.

The guests who gathered around the board of Mr. Thompson were General Hastings, Hon. Walter Lyons, Major Orlady, Hon. C. F. Warwick, General James W. Latta, Hon. C. L. Magee, Al. J. Edwards, Esq., Charles E. Howell, Esq., and others. The other members of the party, which included Congressman George F. Huff, Hon. Marriott Brosius, Hon. George Von Bonhurst, and distinguished guests from Pittsburg, were entertained by Hon. James S. McKean and his sister at their beautiful home adjoining.

The other notable social events comprised dinners by Gen. Frank Reeder, of Easton; ex-Lieutenant Governor William T. Davies, of Towanda; Hon. C. L. Magee, of Pittsburg; Col. James H. Lambert, of Philadelphia; Mr. John Simpson, of Oil City, and Congressman George F. Huff, of Greensburg.

Behind the Scenes.

BEHIND THE SCENES.

IN an old-fashioned house on Walnut street, Philadelphia, with a front that was architecturally fashionable thirty years ago, there sat from the beginning of the campaign to its successful end a man from whose office chair radiated lines of communication to every election precinct in the State of Pennsylvania. To this one man was entrusted the conduct of the campaign for the Republican party, so full of vast possibilities, so pre-eminent in success. Day after day, night after night, this man and his efficient aids kept telegraphers, typewriters, special messengers, secretaries and pasters and folders busy. He rested not, and he gave nobody else any rest—not even the candidates. He was the Czar of the campaign. His name was B. F. Gilkeson, Chairman of the Republican State Committee.

No name was so familiar, so often on the lips of the campaigners, as that of Gilkeson. He was alternately congratulated and condemned. Many a speaker, eloquent, popular and efficient, to whom ten days in the company of the Hastings party was a liberal education, had his anticipations of political pleasure rudely dispelled by a ten word telegram, brief and pointed, which read something like this :

"Leave Hastings' party and go to Weller's Cross Roads. Big meeting there Thursday night. You will be principal speaker.

"Gilkeson."

Then there would be a curse, a sigh, a hurried meal to catch a train, and the spellbinder was off for Weller's Cross Roads, a hundred and fifty

HON. B. F. GILKESON.

miles away, perhaps, as the crow flies. But B. F. Gilkeson was oblivious alike to compliments or objurgation. He had conducted the special campaign in which Galusha A. Grow had been elected by the greatest majority in the State. He was working now to outdo the Grow majority, and the great world of politics knows that Chairman Gilkeson did not labor in vain. He did what he thought would win votes, unconscious and uncaring of what men thought or said of him.

The personality of Mr. Gilkeson is interesting. He is short and stoutly built, ruddy featured, bald, shining head, short brown moustache, and a quick imperious manner. He had resources that men learned of to their sorrow.

"Mr. Chairman, that man X——, the candidate for Senate in our district, is a confounded fool. We are afraid he is going to hurt the Congressional ticket. We want you to send somebody to tell him so."

"Certainly, certainly," said the State Chairman, smiling and turning his eyes ceilingward, while he held his arms close to his side, with both index fingers pointing straight ahead, a fashion he has when he is deep in thought.

"Certainly! good idea; you go and tell him what you think of him, and come back and let me know the result."

That was the last of the kicker.

Mr. Gilkeson is a lawyer; senior member of the firm of Gilkeson & Wright; stands at the head of the Bucks County Bar—his home, a happy one with wife and three children, is at Bristol—and is more proud of his profession than he is of his political triumphs. His love of his profession is the keynote of his unqualified success at the bar.

During the rebellion Mr. Gilkeson was a member of Company I, Seventeenth Regiment, Pennsylvania Militia, the emergency men of 1862, under command of Major John F. Reynolds. He was Second Comptroller of the Treasury of the United States under President Harrison, a position of distinction which he filled with honor to himself and his party.

All that he has ever said for publication on the subject of his real work as chairman of the State Committee, he said to the writer at the close of the campaign: "And I have always regarded attention to every detail as being the keynote to political success, and hence have conducted the last three campaigns during which I have been chairman upon that principle. I have also always regarded it to be of paramount importance that our friends, the enemy, should never know the least thing in reference to our plans, and the campaigns over which I have had the honor to preside have been conducted upon the policy of absolute secrecy. I never permitted myself to indulge in talk about what was to be done or to permit myself to get into the newspapers in interviews, if possible.

"A political campaign, in my judgment, is like a battle; you cannot afford to let the enemy know what is going on in your own camp; hence the maxim, 'do not talk,' has always been my watchword.

"I was ably assisted both in this and the last two campaigns by Jere B. Rex and A. D. Fetterolf, the secretaries of the State Committee, who are entitled to the thanks of the party for their untiring devotion to its interests."

THIS is a story about Charlie Warwick, Henry Hall and the "Indian God." It started up about the greasy head-waters of the Allegheny. It began with the expression of a brakeman in a railroad train, and ended in a shout of enthusiasm from 3000 throats at the greatest mass meeting Greensburg ever saw. It was on the way down the Allegheny Valley Railroad to Kittanning. As the train sped along beside the shining length of the placid river below Franklin, a brakeman approached the group in the smoking car and said:

"We are passing the celebrated sculptured rocks. Long before the white men reached this region the Indians cut figures on these rocks beside the river. There is one that is called the Indian God."

Everybody was all attention in an instant. Noses were flattened against the car window panes, though nothing of the weird character of these monuments of the forgotten and savage sculptor could be seen beyond the broken outlines of the rocks amid the bushes. The occurrence gave rise to a general and more or less learned and animated discussion on Aborigines. In the midst of it Harry Hall lurched up through the swaying car, with a cigarette between his left fore-finger and thumb and a request for a match.

"That Indian God back there," he said, as he tossed the bit of burned wood aside, and dropped carelessly on the arm of Warwick's seat, "reminds me of a story." Then he inflated his lungs with four cubic feet of Sweet Caporal smoke, lifted his eyes dreamily to the dun-colored ceiling of the car, and began :

"There used to live up here in Venango County—I think it was Venango—a big, raw-boned, brunette, whose name I have forgotten. The neighbors nicknamed him the Indian God. When the war broke out he enlisted, and because of his size and his splendid physique, and not on account of his beauty, he was made color sergeant of his regiment. He was a regular dare-devil.

"One day the regiment was ordered into battle, and the color guard started on ahead. They had not gone very far until, for some reason, the regiment was halted. The color guard did not hear the command but went parading on out until they were three hundred feet nearer the enemy than the regimental line. The Colonel got mad and yelled in a voice that could be heard all over the field : 'Halt, there ! Bring those colors back to the regiment.'

"The 'Indian God' halted, turned around, surveyed the situation and yelled back in a voice like a steam calliope :

"'You go to the devil ! Bring your blamed old regiment up to the colors.'"

Hall told the story as only he can tell a story. Everybody roared. After the laugh had subsided Warwick turned to the member in front of him, and with a chuckle said, as he tugged at his moustache :

"Good story, eh ? Devilish good story, ain't it ? I'm going to use that." Then he curled himself up with his knees braced against the seat in front and on a level with the top of his head, and for the next hour did not speak a word, but sat gazing intently out of the window, where trees and barns and cattle went swimming past the train. Occasionally his lips would move. Hall put it, "Charley is thinking what he is going to say next."

There was not a hint of the "Indian God" story in the City Solicitor's speech that night, nor the next night, nor the next. Saturday we were at Greensburg. Old Westmoreland was in the throes of a new political parturition, and the streets of her county town were black with people, while the Roman candle balls and rocket stars made polka-dots on the blackness of the sky.

There was a magnificent audience in the court house, and a magnificent but mad crowd outside that could not get in.

Warwick was the first speaker and he was in excellent voice, with the inspiration of Colonel Huff's dinner table behind him. He was never in better condition. A number of old soldiers, some with Grand Army badges on their coats, were scattered through the audience. Warwick spoke for forty minutes, and then came his peroration. It was the "Indian God" story, with the Indian God left out. And what a metamorphosis! He described the gallant son of Pennsylvania, who, when his country called, obeyed her voice. He carried his audience by the force of his eloquence and imagination into Virginia where, thirty-three years ago, the army of the North stretched itself along the valley of the Potomac like an irresistible barrier to the northward flow of secession's tide. Then one night the order to prepare for conflict went round among the marshaled host, and in the morning, ere the fadeless fire of the stars had disappeared before the coming of the day, the columns were in array, and the rising sun looked down on a battle line of blue, fringed with a ribbon of glittering steel. Then the advance! the color guard in front. A halt! the color guard marches on. A strip of gray breaks through a distant belt of foliage. The enemy is moving.

"Halt!" shouts the Colonel. "Bring those colors back to the regiment." The stalwart sergeant turns. His eye sweeps the intervening distance, just as a puff of smoke and the dull boom of a gun from a masked battery behind the gray advance breaks on the hush of the morning air. As the smoke wreath mounts upward like a frightened dove, the dauntless color sergeant replies in words that go ringing down the line:

"I cannot, Colonel. This flag never goes backward. For God's sake, bring your regiment up to the colors!"

The audience had been hanging on the speaker's words. As he concluded, pandemonium broke loose. The court room rang with repeated cheers and the old soldier in the background, with a livid sabre scar on his cheek, flung his Grand Army cap half-way to the ceiling and yelled above the whirling din: "Glory Hallelujah!"

SPEAKING of hand shaking, a favorite cant expression of Orlady, Warwick and Schaffer was "De glad hand, an' de marble heart." It came about this way:

At one of the towns, Bradford or DuBois, or somewhere up there, an inebriated but hilarious citizen, his manly bosom bedecked with badges of all colors to match his breath, came rolling up to one of the candidates.

"Shake," he exclaimed, as he tilted his hat over his left eyebrow with his left hand.

"Oh, I'm onter ye," he exclaimed, with a leer and a wave of his left hand, holding on to the candidate with his right as he did a fore-and-aft movement with his unsteady body.

"I'm onter ye," he repeated with a wag of his head, the leer growing into a grin, as he waved his hand aimlessly around.

"Youse fellers is aroun' now givin' us de glad hand; after 'leckshun's over youse'l be givin' us de marble heart. See?" Then gathering himself together for a supreme effort, and hitching at his waistband with both hands he exclaimed, with a self-satisfied grin:

"But what's th' odds? Who cares? Look at th' fun we're havin'. Who-o o-p-e-e," and he moved on to make room for the next man, who was sober.

THOUGH identified with the campaign in many unostentatious ways, General Frank Reeder, Secretary of the Commonwealth, is deserving of a place in this work for other reasons than that. His varied services as a public man, his genial temperament and his elevated character have long rendered him a conspicuous figure in State Republican politics. General Reeder is a lawyer by profession, born at Easton, is in his forty-ninth year, and is a son of the first Governor of Kansas Territory. Andrew Reeder. He left Princeton College when seventeen years old and enlisted as a private in the Fifth Pennsylvania Regiment. He served throughout the war, coming out as a brevet-brigadier general, having commanded a brigade before he was of age. He was associated in law practice with Chester A. Arthur in New York. President Grant appointed General Reeder the Eleventh District Internal Revenue Collector in 1873. The General commanded the Fifth Brigade of the old National Guard, and is an ex-commander of the Pennsylvania Department of the Grand Army. He was a delegate to the Republican National Conventions of 1888 and 1892, ran for Congress against Howard Mutchler in 1893, and was the predecessor of Colonel Gilkeson as chairman of the Republican State Committee.

GENERAL FRANK REEDER,
Secretary of the Commonwealth.

THE CURTIN FUNERAL.

THE CURTIN FUNERAL.

IT was a great but gloomy day for Bellefonte. The white angel above the fountain in the Court House Square seemed to drop a benediction from its outstretched, pulseless hand, over the solemn pageant that passed before its sightless eyes when Pennsylvania's great war Governor went to his final abiding place in the little cemetery in the shadow of Bald Eagle Mountain.

It seemed as though time had turned a leaf in his voiceless record of the past; as though the days of the war years were here again and the rhythmict ramp of marching men, the roll of drums and rattle of caisson and gun carriage on the highways were but incidents to a review of Lincoln's minute men by the virile and courageous war Governor of the Commonwealth of William Penn. But the wisp of black on the scarlet guidon of Battery B, the crape-wrapped colors of the regiments, the solemn dirge of the brigade band and above all the black casket with the shining folds of the flag draped above the breast of the peaceful figure with its strong, white, classic features lying silent within, told not only the story of Bellefonte's sorrow, but the grief of a great State.

The day began with clouds and showers and the coming of the troops. A little later and the high dignitaries, the representatives of war and peace, Governor Pattison and his cabinet, Adjutant General Greenland and his staff, and older men of other days, ex-United States Senators, members of the Supreme Court, soldiers of the rebellion, the men who with Andrew Gregg Curtin moulded the history of a generation ago, came to pay their last tribute to his memory. And the sight that greeted them all was silent shops, deserted industries, empty school-houses, closed stores, emblems of mourning on every residence, flags at half-mast, the populace on the streets.

It was ten o'clock when the Bar Association meeting was called to order in the court house. It was the most distinguished assemblage that ever gathered in Bellefonte. Men were there from every portion of Pennsylvania and from neighboring States. They had come to stand by the open grave of him who had stood like a bulwark for human freedom and the preservation of the Union when the flowing tide of rebellion lapped Pennsylvania's border.

The men who spoke in eulogy of the distinguished dead were reminiscent as became their years. They were pathetic at times, eulogistic always.

As the day grew the shriek of locomotive whistles increased as special train after special train with their loads of mourners or militia swept around the big curve to the city. The streets became crowded first, then well nigh impassable. But in the gray stone house with the wide porch on the main street where for the last years of his life ex-Governor Curtin had lived, all was silent, with drawn blinds, but for the knots of men who came and went with hushed voices. By noon the growing crowd had increased to thousands, that moved to and fro in dense masses on the sidewalk or formed a semi-circle at a distance from the house whose entrance was now guarded by a detachment of troops.

On the stroke of twelve a little company of men emerged from the house carrying between them a black burden. As they passed up the street under the lowering skies the crowd parted on either side. The dull gray court house with its massive pillars wrapped with black never looked so dull and gloomy and forbidding as it did when the body of the ex-Governor was carried in and laid in state in the carpeted area before the judges' stand. There were soldiers on every hand. Guards at the entrances and at the exit. Sentries at the top of the staircases and beside the silent sleeper. Grizzled old Grand Army veterans guarded the floral emblems that were grouped about the bier. There was an elaborate piece from the Free Masons, the insignia of the Grand Army from that organization, a broken column of immortelles from the Bar Association, besides numerous private offerings.

In the hour-and-a-half that elapsed while the body lay in state, an unbroken stream of people entered the front door of the court house, passed around the black casket and emerged in the rear. All classes and conditions of men were in the throng—women and little children were there by hundreds. Mothers lifted their children up that they might look down on that face and never forget it. Many burst into tears and hundreds went their way with swimming eyes. The sodden grass in the court yard was beaten level and worn away by the feet of these thousands of pilgrims of patriotism.

General Hastings and the members of his party who had traveled all night by special train, with a break of three hours sleep at Altoona, reached Bellefonte at ten o'clock. Carriages were in waiting and they were immediately driven to the residence of Mr. Wilbur F. Reeder, the law partner of General Hastings, where they were entertained at lunch by Mr. and Mrs. Reeder.

Then General Hastings walked down to the Court House with Justice Dean. The soldiers on guard presented arms as the pair passed in with uncovered heads and up toward the long black casket. The great jurist halted only an instant, but Hastings paused, and gazed for fully a minute on the set, stern features of his friend. A tear trembled on his cheek; he brushed it hurriedly away and walked back down the aisle again with bowed head. The next moment the undertaker had fastened down the casket lid forever.

Daniel H. Hastings was the last personal friend on earth to look into the white upturned face of the great war Governor of this imperial State.

The arrangements for the obsequies were absolutely perfect. Ex-Governor Beaver was in full charge. In the public square was stationed the famous Second Brigade Band, which faced the brown guns of Battery B on the opposite side of the quadrangle. The Sheridan Troop filled in the remainder of the space, while farther down the street to the south and east there stretched a ribbon of steel and blue which marked the position of the infantry and the State College Cadets.

At 1.30 the body was carried from the court house back to the Gregg mansion where at two o'clock the funeral services were held. The casket was of red cedar covered with black broadcloth, lined with black satin, the plate containing only the name " Andrew Gregg Curtin."

The funeral procession was scheduled to start at three o'clock. At precisely ten minutes of that hour the bandmaster of the brigade saw a sabre lifted into the air by a cavalryman stationed opposite the Curtin home. It was his signal, and the next instant the music of " Nearer My God to Thee" floated out on the chilly air. Up to this time the sky had been heavy with storm clouds which threatened rain, but scarcely had the first bar of the hymn music been played when the sun broke forth with all his radiance, and at this instant the casket was carried out and placed in the waiting hearse. It was the only moment of sunshine during the day.

The grave was lined with evergreen, and the services at its side were according to the ritual of the Grand Army. Only the pall-bearers. the male members of Governor Curtin's family and the Grand Army Committee with the attendant ministers saw the body lowered into the grave. Then after the prayers were finished and the benediction pronounced the mourners and attendants stepped to one side. The thousands who had gathered behind the solemn, protecting line of soldiers stood in silence.

Suddenly there was a low, harsh word of

command, followed by the ominous sound of loading rifles, and then across the open grave there shot a line of fire. Three times was this repeated, and as the firing squads ceased their parting salute, and while the white smoke wreaths had scarcely lifted to the tree tops, the mellow notes of bugle call floated out and up, and in their penetrating sweetness seemed to reach the distant mountain side. It was the call of "lights out," and Andrew Gregg Curtin was left alone forever.

www.ingramcontent.com/pod-product-compliance
Lightning Source LLC
Chambersburg PA
CBHW031451160426
43195CB00010BB/937